To Fletcher!

Blessings to You

[signature]

HISTORY OF THE
ONE TRUE GOD

VOLUME I: THE ORIGIN OF GOOD AND EVIL

GWEN SHAMBLIN

Printed in the United States of America
Remnant Publishing

Weigh Down Ministries ®
308 Seaboard Lane, Franklin, TN 37067
1-800-844-5208
www.weighdown.com

ISBN # 1-892729-14-8

THIS BOOK BELONGS TO:

_____

And there was war in heaven. Michael and his angels fought against the dragon, and the dragon and his angels fought back. But he was not strong enough, and they lost their place in heaven. (Revelation 12:7-8)

Table of Contents

Preface

"Write down the revelation and make it plain on tablets so that a herald may run with it. For the revelation awaits an appointed time; it speaks of the end and will not prove false. Though it linger, wait for it; it will certainly come and will not delay." (Habakkuk 2:2-3)

From 1998 to the year 2001, during the months before and surrounding the beginning years of the Remnant Fellowship Church,[1] a 14 chapter book was written—originally entitled *"The Death of Sovereignty."* The intent of this book was to chronicle history from the ongoing Spiritual War of the Heavens with Satan, to the earthly war of lies on Adam and Eve, to the establishment of Jerusalem. The book continues with brief overview of church and religious history to the present religious state of America. It ends with the rise of the New Jerusalem. The concentration is on the historical cycle of nations and religions as they obeyed or disobeyed and the resulting effect on their rise and fall. The chapters were stored in the Weigh Down Archives and some of the chapters were used in various video series.

Over a decade later, in a recent prompting, the pages were dusted off and updated and the multi-volume series title was changed to *"History of the ONE TRUE GOD,"* while "The Death of Sovereignty" remained the subtitle of a latter Volume.

In a miraculously short five weeks, God allowed the publication of Volume One as well as the filming of six corresponding videos—effortlessly—and that only being specified to emphasize that it is not me, but rather God pouring out the effort and inspiration.

There is much hypocrisy in the religious world today as evidenced by the ever-increasing number of various religions and denominations emerging on the horizon, as well as the unprecedented number of churches closing their doors—a number as large as 3,500 to 4,000 per year according to the latest Barna Study.[2] The Great Dragon called Satan has been busy for centuries, so many churches are either dead or appear alive but have lost their purpose as they now concentrate on transforming earthly governments over advancing the Kingdom of God—forgetting that mere Christianity teaches us that by saving (seeking) the government of God first, everything else will be added to us. This country is in desperate need for a God-first revival and the Truth that Christ spoke of that sets men free from his own personal devices.

---

1   www.RemnantFellowship.org
2   www.barna.org

The purpose of the multi-volume series *History of the ONE TRUE GOD* is not to publish one more book to add to the overwhelming confusion in the sea of "religious" literature. This country has produced countless amounts of literature, missionaries, ministries, televangelists, Christian music artists, and now the sky-rocketing cloud of religious websites, video streaming, and YouTube channels. America has more steeples than any other country in the world. No, it was not for a void of "religious" literature, but rather a need for a different approach—for indeed, there is a distinction between religion and True Religion. Had these contributions tamed the pride, the lust, and the greed in the heart of man, there would be no need for anything and our churches and our governments would not be at risk. But the rapid rise in greed and self-indulgence verifies that there is an unfortunate form of religion that dominates America but has no power…"a form of godliness but denying its power."[1]

The main purpose of this book is to expose false religion. Too much of history is penned from the twisted perspective of man, but *History of the ONE TRUE GOD* is humbly scripted from the standpoint of God. For example, instead of answering the hard questions from man's perspective—questions concerning God's wrath, His holy separated people, the authenticity of His Word, the actuality of the flood, the church, the Laws, the Commands, the religious wars, the deadly disasters and the death of the innocent—the hard questions disappear as they are answered from God's viewpoint, as quickly as taking the plank out of your own eye gives you vision for the reality of others. This book emphasizes the breaking heart of The Creator and defends God as the only Being who wants all men to live forever. It points the responsibility back on the heart of man rather than blaming the benevolent Creator of All. Once one sees through the lies of Satan and his powerful delusion[2] and grasps the depth of the personalized love of God through history, it erases the doubt and you find the faith and missing power to be born again that comes only in True Religion. You know when you read it and run with it, for it transforms you from being downhearted to a victorious Saint filled with inexpressible joy. This fundamental and essential Truth from the Heavens provides needed answers and direction, for God is trying to equip the Saints and prepare us for a future experience that will not delay.

Satan has deceived many and God has been shortchanged. It is time to rally the troops, and what better way than to learn from history so that it will not be repeated.

All overdue glory to The One True God, The LORD God Almighty, and His Son, Jesus Christ who is at His right hand... May His Kingdom come and His will be done on Earth as it is in Heaven.

---

1   II Timothy 3:5
2   II Thessalonians 2:11

The Fallen Angel...
The Beginning of Evil

CHAPTER 1

A long, long time ago, before the beginning of terrestrial time on Earth, there was The One Omnipotent Being... The Great I Am—The Most High God. He always had existed—infinite and omnipresent—the Only and the Sovereign, for there was no other existence or matter in the vast expanse. The clearest title for this being was "The Source." Since this Sole Source of all matter was pure holiness, goodness, and righteousness, He had a presence that was blinding—wrapped in a garment of radiance, which could be seen for millions of light years. He sat high above the stars of the Universe. He was The Source of all wisdom[1] and knowledge, The Source of every subject matter from physics, math, and engineering to... science and physiology and medicine.

---

1   Job 12:13

Yes, **The Source** held all knowledge and wisdom as if He was a mainframe computer or brain, but in this cerebral sea of intellect there existed another phenomenon called love. **The Most High Source of All** housed both *wisdom* and *love*.[1] A brain with a heart—this phenomenal coexistence of all intellect and loving emotion proved His perfection. The blend of wisdom and love was flawless, for after all, if the intellect had overridden compassion, it would have created a god that was a dictator of legalism. On the other hand, if the emotion had overridden wisdom, it would have been a god who directed creation down a path of decay and self-destruction—a spoiler. But **The Great I Am** had the perfect amalgamation of love and wisdom that produced a self-regeneration of which I call the *life force*.

Not only did this Omnipotent Source held the secret to His own youth, but out of His generosity, He created other beings and extended this invaluable life force to other created beings.

THE LIFE FORCE

This *life force* was self-perpetuating light, life, and beauty—in other words, the secret to eternity. It is one thing to create life, but another to keep it going. **The One and Only God** had the secret formula that gave the victory over death. Many think of eternity as a span of time, but eternity is simply existence without death. Not only did this **Omnipotent Source** hold the secret to His own youth, but out of His generosity, He created other beings and extended this invaluable

---

1   I John 4:16

life force to other created beings. His Only Son was the firstborn over all creation.[1] During the beginning, though invisible, all of creation looked for and depended upon The Source for the essential, eternal life force, and therefore there was peace and there

The secret of this life-force was due to the perpetual, reciprocal love and provisions of The Creator to the created, and in return, the uninterrupted, complete link of the created due to appreciation. The creatures were almost buoyant with effervescent joy.

was love—in other words…"one TRUE RELIGION."

God was so supremely beautiful that no one questioned or challenged His position. Everyone knew they could not compete with the resources, power, wisdom, and love of The Source—nor did they have a desire to compete. It made no sense, for it was impossible. So for centuries, The One True God was the uncontested Monarch and the CEO of the Universe. His Kingdom and Angelic Staff were immense. Loved and beloved, The Great CEO ran His Kingdom with the best perks, bonuses, and retirement plans. This business was second to none in production, for there were no antagonists in this unified and glorious Kingdom of Love which spanned from one star to another.

Time had not been invented, and all that creatures knew was eternity. It was all because of the secret of this life force extended from The Creator to the Created. The secret of this life force was due to

---

1   *Colossians 1:15*

the perpetual, reciprocal love and provisions that The Creator gave the Created, and in return, the uninterrupted, complete link of love the Created gave back due to appreciation. Love—derived from appreciation—was *the connection.* All of the Angels experienced this priceless, constant continuum of energized life—never ending and unfaltering, always deepening, strengthening between The Creator and the Created Beings like roots in the ground. You could feel the ever-intensifying love *connection* because of the increase in adoration, increase in gentle kindness, controlled patience, and profound peace. The Created longed to imitate the goodness of The Creator. Since the creation had been given the secret of vivacity and were full of this Divine Spirit, they all had an energy and a vitality that was full of enthusiasm and exuberance. The creatures were almost buoyant with effervescent joy. The entire joyous setting was way beyond description and imagination using the human language.[1]

Keep in mind, terminology such as pride, vanity, conceit, envy, greed, evil, antiauthority, termination, and unemployment were non-existent. They were unknown concepts. Due to the unbelievable generosity of God that was beyond compare, in this Kingdom there was no question of whom all Angels and Staff owed allegiance to. With song and praise and worship and hands lifted high, appreciation was the only word on the tip of every creature's tongue.[2] It was incomprehensible for all Created Beings not to give all of their heart, mind, soul, and strength to God, due to the massive debt that all created beings owed The Creator. How could you ever repay the opportunity to exist and then pay for the ongoing high price of the *life force* electricity that is offered for infinity? The meter readings and electric bills were too pricey for any created being to repay.

---

1   *Hebrews 12:22*
2   *Revelation 7:11*

THE HOLY MANUAL

As in all organizations, this Heavenly company had an *Employee Manual* and these precious, ancient words were crystal clear, essential, and priceless. They went as follows...

> ### Heavenly Employee Manual:
>
> The Lord God is One. There are no other gods (sources of life) before Him. Angels are created beings. Life is a gift, and since created beings are not sources, they need to connect to The Source. If you want to live and live forever, you must stay connected to the One True God—your life force. The Connection (God's Spirit) supplies the guidance for daily life and the electricity—the life force—for eternal life. Appreciation births love for The Creator, and love connects the Created to The Creator. Do not let anything interrupt this connection to the only Source of life—God Almighty. Above all, shun life-threatening pride and self-sufficiency. If you disconnect from The Source, you will die.

To any Angel reading *The Holy Manual*, they would automatically know that appreciation and loving obedience were the visible signs that your connection was complete. Therefore, obedience and appreciation were monitored. But appreciation to God was the most celebrated of all characteristics, for it was the substance that set off this chain of reactions. Since this Holy Directive was true, the reverse of this directive was also true…

- If you lose the focus and forget that God is The Source of All, then you will lose the appreciation.
- If you do not appreciate all you have been given through this connection, you will lose the love.
- If you lose the love, you will lose *the Connection* to life.
- Once unplugged from the only Source of electricity, you will die.

Disobedience and less praise on the lips (for example, neglecting the ongoing adoration services) were the signs and symptoms that were monitored to see if there were any bad connections. So the goal would be to let nothing interrupt the flow of love. You would know that the electricity was gone, for your energy would be diminished, your mind confused, your joy decreased, and your light of obedience would flicker.

Pride was the enemy, for it tempted the Created to appreciate self above God and believe that they were self-reliant. Even though believing you were a source was a seemingly impossible thought process, pride was the one thing that could cause a created being to unplug—a force to be reckoned with. Therefore, every aspect of pride was studied so it could be shunned. In addition, every detail of humility was studied so it could be imitated. The Angelic beings could not comprehend wanting praise from one another. All praise belonged to God. However, The One True God taught the Angels to Honor those who honored Him.

Love of created things over The Creator could cause electrical shorts in the energized lifeline—spiritual surges. Even though

14

a created being could possibly reboot the system, these *life force* surges would cause damage to *the Connection. The Connection* was everything if you wanted to live forever, so it was clear that you protected *the Connection* above all things and at all costs—so all dependent creatures kept all of their mind and heart on 𝕿𝖍𝖊 𝕱𝖆𝖙𝖍𝖊𝖗 𝖔𝖋 𝕬𝖑𝖑. Pride was the most avoided substance of all substances. Even the thought of pride struck fear into the hearts of Beings, for they did not want to be disconnected.

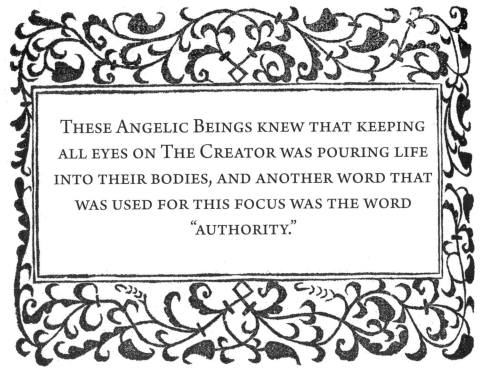

THESE ANGELIC BEINGS KNEW THAT KEEPING ALL EYES ON THE CREATOR WAS POURING LIFE INTO THEIR BODIES, AND ANOTHER WORD THAT WAS USED FOR THIS FOCUS WAS THE WORD "AUTHORITY."

Notice that the *Employee Manual* was written strictly for the good of the employee, and so 100 percent of all commands and directives were made not to benefit 𝕿𝖍𝖊 𝕮𝖗𝖊𝖆𝖙𝖔𝖗, but for the benefit of the Created—all priceless secrets to the gift of life. These Angelic Beings knew that keeping all eyes on 𝕿𝖍𝖊 𝕮𝖗𝖊𝖆𝖙𝖔𝖗 was pouring life into their bodies. Another word for keeping all eyes on 𝕿𝖍𝖊 𝕮𝖗𝖊𝖆𝖙𝖔𝖗 was "authority line." It was impossible for everyone to be close to The Creator, so the younger and less experienced ones had to focus on the older and wiser Beings above them. So this authority line was *the Connection* to The Father. Now the Angels were connected also to each other and worked arm to arm, shoulder to shoulder. And *the Connection* to The Father was stronger as all the Angels unified with each other, making a strong impenetrable bond, like an incredibly thick wall of brick and mortar—a swarm of locusts, a herd of buffalo—nothing could break the unity of THE KINGDOM OF CONNECTIONS, which all centered around The Source. The Heavens cherished both authority and unity, because it just made *the Connection* to God stronger and the fruit of peace and joy greater, and it deepened the love and appreciation for this one and only Selfless Life Source. This secure connection promised eternal life.

THE EMERGENCE OF PRIDE

Now over an unnamed length of time—the first span of infinity—there rose up in the company a charismatic employee named LUCIFER.[1] He had been advanced and promoted to a high supervisory, general management position, therefore many eyes were on him as he looked to The Great I Am. He was given affectionate titles such as "Morning Star" and "The Dawn of Light."[2]

At some point in timeless age, even though it was veiled, a horrifying thing happened… a generation arose that failed to encourage the younger generation to read the *Employee Manual*. It had been put to the side, so this new generation was unaware of the life-

---

1   Isaiah 14:12 KJV
2   Isaiah 14:12

The Connection was everything if you wanted to live forever, so it was clear that you protected the Connection above all things and at all costs.

threatening danger of pride and indeed did not know what it looked like. So a single seed of pride was allowed to linger in the heart of the great LUCIFER. As the pride took root, the eyes of his mind and heart would wander away from The Creator. And as one thing always leads to another, the wayward thoughts mixed with pride conjured up a depraved notion—a theory that God had everyone focus up and obey Him for His own personal advancement. LUCI-FER thought the following: "What would it be like to just be free to do your own thing? Why else would God have given us a separate brain?" And because of this completely opposite theory, he had a hypothesis that this death that was referred to in the *Employee Manual* was simply an unsubstantiated, unproven threat used simply to maintain absolute authority. In addition, humility was something just to make Beings cower. Believing that the intimidation of the threat of death was groundless, baseless, and really altogether unjustified, he rejected the required appreciation of God, which led to a growing concept of antiauthority. He twisted the ancient TRUTH that "authority is simply an open door—an opportunity to connect to God" to the lie... "authority is an opportunity *for* God." He now saw God as being selfish—a ridiculous thought, but a side effect of pride nevertheless. LUCIFER began to experiment with unplugging from The Source, something that no one dared try. In the beginning, he tested this with short disconnections, which led to increased pride and self-reliance. It built up to longer increments of time until eventually the prideful arrogance blossomed and he did the unthinkable and unplugged from the will of God like a terminal would unplug from a mainframe computer.

In these experiments, he did not readily notice that he was unplugged from God's electricity and Spirit because he replaced those sensations with a wicked electricity called lust. This lust burned inside, and he experienced a greed for money and power. This burning lust, somewhat like God's life force, had its own self-perpetuation but instead of giving life like the life force, it destroyed the insides of the angels. Once unplugged, LUCIFER felt insatiable greed for the praise of the created rather than the Old CEO. The lust would burn and rise up in his throat, and it felt good as long as it was fulfilled. But what LUCIFER did not know or count on was that there was a huge difference between the electricity from God and the burning from the lust. God's source filled you up more and more until you felt like you had too much—your cup was overflowing. But the lust sensation was never satisfied—you always felt high for a moment and then later very depressed, so you needed more and more to get rid of the empty feelings that it created. So LUCIFER went from the life force to a LUST–FORCE.

But LUCIFER was on an insurrection mission, and he kept himself busy so that he did not notice the disconnection. Certain skills seemed instinctive to him, such as using divisiveness to divide and conquer, thus forming his own following. He intuitively knew to separate unsuspecting Angels from the TRUTH of God and from His *Heavenly Manual* by interrupting their focus on God. He shrewdly knew to plant seeds of discontent about their circumstances, and he assured them that they would not surely die[1] and that God did not really care about all that fuss and connection and focus stuff anyway. "God was *way* too important for all that—He had more important things to do." It was such a terrible lie, for it robbed the unsuspecting angels of their <u>purpose</u>! Under the guise of concern... slander and sweet-tasting gossip poured from his lips—slander of God and His loyal, unbendable Angels.

While the loyal Angels focused on the love of God, LUCIFER lust-

---

1   *Genesis 3:4*

ed after God's position—Angels were in awe of God, LUCIFER was in awe of himself. So in his heart he deceived himself and said, *"I will ascend to heaven; I will raise my throne above the stars of God; I will sit enthroned on the mount of assembly, on the utmost heights of the sacred mountain. I will ascend above the tops of the clouds; I will make myself like the Most High." (Isaiah 14:13-14)*

How could people be so foolish to believe they are the source and they can contend with their Creator? What LUCIFER failed to realize was that the consequence of unplugging did indeed cut off the life giving Electricity, and the first thing to go was the sight. Blindness to TRUTH was almost instant once unplugged. This was no ordinary blindness—it was a prideful blindness, which is the worst of all. Prideful blindness boasts it can see when it cannot see at all. However, with pride, the brain hallucinates and conjures up its own visions and interpretations.[1] LUCIFER was living a lie, so he made up his own destructive rules and directives for himself and his followers.

With his sight eradicated, he could not see the death process.[2] He could not see himself accurately in the mirror any longer. No longer able to tap into the blood of life from the Heavens, at first he did not notice his organs shutting down, the necrosis and atrophying of all tissues, and the emergence of cancerous cells that were metastasizing all over his body and leaving scars on his face. Blinded now and numb to the transfer from the life force to the LUST-FORCE, he was becoming accustomed to constant pain from the various dysfunctional conditions. With dementia setting in, his mind started playing tricks on him, so he felt unfounded fears and paranoia and panic attacks, along with increasing distrust and jealousy

---

1   *Isaiah 6:9, Matthew 13:14*

2   *John 15:1, 5-6*

and malice. In the night, Saints could hear the moans and cries[1] from the antiauthority demons having terrifying nightmares. It was so disconcerting, for all prior nights from the beginning of creation had been wrapped in the most beautiful, indescribable, comfortable, snuggly linens and the sweetest of sleep and divine dreams from this relationship with The God of Love.[2] Again, the eyes that were once 20/20—full of the light of the Truth of God prior to the rebellion—were now seeing only darkness and their own hallucinations. The ears that could hear Truth were becoming deaf to reality and only lies could be discerned. Where soft, forgiving love once ruled in the heart, it was now replaced with outbursts of anger, depression, and stone-cold hate[3]—expressions absolutely non-existent, nor seen in Heaven before.

Even though most of the death process was internal, Lucifer's looks were rapidly changing… he was unaware of the increasing sensations of emptiness, anger, malice, envy, and jealousy. Those who followed Satan were also rapidly aging, and the decay brought with it an offensive aroma that lingered around the rebellious. At first, they were lurking in the darkness and hid away.

But the worst curse of all from unplugging was the death to the mind—reasoning, logic, and analysis. The sad part of prideful blindness is that you cannot see yourself in the mirror, so you fail to see the need to change. The other sad part of this unusual blindness is that you spend all of your time on how *others* need to

---

1   II Peter 2:4
2   I John 4:16
3   Matthew 24:10-12

change—you become a projectionist. The now irrational LUCIFER blamed all of his self-induced pain and curses onto The CEO. LUCIFER accused The CEO of being oppressive and enslaving, while blind to the fact that SATAN was the tyrant who loved no one but himself—running over others to get where he wanted, climbing up the ladder. He used these lies to gain a following. SATAN did not just unplug himself, he talked other angels into unplugging from the Mainframe Computer and fooled himself into believing that he was doing his subjects a favor—yet in reality, he was giving all of his fellow angels a death sentence. The unplugged demons turned to lust and some became obese, some drunk, some diseased from sexual lust, and some warped from narcissism. But LUCIFER—the demon of demons—lusted after the praise of Angels. LUCIFER was starting to wrinkle from death to his cells, the smile on his face was transformed into a frown, the crown on his head was turning into horns,[1] his voice was more coarse and shrill, and his speech never ceased to vomit up lies. In short, those unplugged were distorted. Even though LUCIFER had become the very picture of shriveled death, he strutted around to prove that he was very much alive—in an attempt to validate his theory that death was merely a false threat. More and more angels bought into his lies.

Lucifer was starting to wrinkle from death to his cells, the smile on his face was transformed into a frown, the crown on his head was turning into horns.

---

1   *Revelation 17:7*

THE INSURRECTION

A great chasm was forming in the Heavens, for since the beginning of time the only thing that the Angels had ever feared was losing sight of the smile of their loving Creator. Disapproval from God or having His face turn from them was to be avoided at all costs. The Connection was everything. But now as the self-importance rose in the ranks, these unplugged angels—now demons—feared the face of God. The rebellious were now just as blind as LUCIFER and did not know that they were bowing down to The GRIM REAPER. In their pain, they convinced themselves that they were victims, and they joined the campaign against the Heavens. The seasoned, concerned, loving Archangels tried to warn SATAN and his angels by pointing out the obvious evidence of decay and signs of reversal of life, but they were met with mockery, jeers, insults, and flaming arrows, for these demons could not see the light of TRUTH any longer.

Try though the Archangels may, the Loyal Staff could not penetrate the prideful blindness. So into this beautiful city of peace... factions and dissensions and discord erupted, all because of one seed of the most diabolical substance in existence—pride.

Pride had the power to deceive even Angels into believing that they were capable of successfully disengaging from The Creator. Pride had changed "The Morning Star" into a new nickname, "The DRAGON" [1] or "SERPENT." The now insane DEVIL believed the impossible—that he was equal to or greater than The CEO. The DRAGON would boldly sit in the Boss' chair—His throne. [2] It made SATAN feel more powerful. Here he would create new laws that he claimed were freeing—yet in reality, they were enslaving each angel to his

---

1   *Revelation 12:3*
2   *Isaiah 14:13-14*

lust and love of self. Totalitarianism was a concept he hated when God ruled, but a pleasing concept if he was on the throne. Like all leaders not connected to this Loving, Life-Giving Source, LUCIFER became a tyrant and used created beings to their detriment. It was his theory that God had used created beings to extend God's life, therefore God instated dictatorship, repression, subjugation, and cruelty.

In his spare time, LUCIFER prepared a speech to convince The Sovereign CEO that a shared partnership would be superior. And he felt like if he could get enough followers to back him up, that The CEO would be convinced that His ancient business ideas were obsolete and that the youthful and fresh ideas of employee empowerment and shared power and authority were indeed the new and superior way to run the Kingdom.

But little did SATAN know that he was wasting his time—God would never allow this reversal of authority to enter the Heavens and The Source was never going to deny Himself—not because He was greedy for power like LUCIFER thought, but because of a concept LUCIFER could not even comprehend. It was because God never wanted to cut off the lifeline to any created beings. He wanted each Angel to live forever. Surrendering to rebellion would mean the death of each angel.

GOD FIGHTS BACK

God had tried with everything He had to extend this secret, perfect blend of love and wisdom that brought life, love, and freedom to all His Angels, including His long loved "Son of Dawn," and now He found that His loving efforts were twisted into accusations of selfish, controlling pressure. The lies about God were working. The deeper the love and the bigger the heart one has, the greater the pain. The wise and loving Source of All was in the greatest pain. Yet to spare the loyal Remnant of Angels, God stood His ground... *"And there was war in heaven. Michael and his angels fought against the dragon, and the dragon and his angels fought back. But he was not strong enough, and they lost their place in heaven. The great dragon was hurled down—that ancient serpent called the devil, or Satan, who leads the whole world astray. He was hurled to the earth, and his angels with him."*[1]

LUCIFER had wanted to rise above the throne and the stars of God, but Isaiah explained[2]... *"How you have fallen from heaven, O morning star, son of the dawn! You have been cast down to the earth, you who once laid low the nations! You said in your heart, 'I will ascend to heaven; I will raise my throne above the stars of God; I will sit enthroned on the mount of assembly, on the utmost heights of the sacred mountain. I will ascend above the tops of the clouds; I will make myself like the Most High.' But you are brought down to the grave, to the depths of the pit."*

---

1   Revelation 12:7-9
2   Isaiah 14:12-15

The entrance of one seed of pride had changed many things in the Heavens. The greatest damage done to the Universe by the entrance of pride was the twisting of the picture of the essential, loving authority line which supplied the Electricity. Where it was once pictured as the Graceful, Omnipotent, Merciful, and Beautiful God doting over the every need of the created—a helping hand guiding and fixing and healing all needs, like a devoted mother to a child—authority had turned into a picture of an insensitive, enslaving dictator. Yes, there was a rejoicing in Heaven to eradicate the pride... *"But woe to the earth and the sea, because the devil has gone down to you! He is filled with fury, because he knows that his time is short."*[1]

Time did not exist—but since death entered the Universe, the clock started ticking and terrestrial time began. SATAN was sentenced to the abyss of eternal hellfire. So the fuming FALLEN ANGEL was hurled to the Earth, convinced that The CEO's business, Kingdom, Incorporated, would go under without him, and he left feeling secure enough in his abilities and secure enough in being able to win the Earth over—if they were free will agents with freedom to make their own choices. Inspired by his own pride, he started his own business, called Deceit, Incorporated. One of the most obnoxious things about those who are unplugged is that they unashamedly copy and plagiarize and make a counterfeit reproduction of everything. So SATAN copied as much as he could to mimic Heaven, Incorporated. This is the origin of counterfeit religions.

Knowing that his sentence was irreversible, doom inevitable, and his time limited, he challenged The Great I Am a second time, but now with confidence to win man. This was the origin of good and now evil and hate—a hate that would not stop until the Lake of Fire was filled to the brim, because misery loves company. ✺

---

1   Revelation 12:12

This was the origin of good and now evil and hate—a hate that would not stop until the Lake of Fire was filled to the brim, because misery loves company.

Unfortunately, pride comes in so many forms and is so transmittable that it did not take long for Lucifer to convert many angels against their God, as one by one they cut off the umbilical cord that fed them. These antiauthority agents organized a war to capture the Throne of God, because they erroneously believed that the life force was housed in the Throne itself.

From the Stars to the Earth

CHAPTER 2

T here had been an immeasurable length of peace in the Heavens before the rebellion. But the rebellion came on fast and the battle was furious.[1] The perfect, white canvas of the eternal Heavens—which was full of love—was splashed with black, as the evil, diabolical spirit of anger and hate was birthed. The angel who had once been called the "Son of Dawn"—and who had been meticulously hovered over by the broad, protective wings of The Creator—had unplugged and transformed into a thoroughly cynical being.

A contagious deadly virus called pride (I am and therefore I deserve) entered the Heavens through the heart of SATAN. Unfortunately, pride comes in so many forms and is so transmittable that it did not take long for LUCIFER to convert many angels and turn them

---

1   Revelation 12:7-9

against their God, as one by one they cut off the umbilical cord that fed them. These antiauthority agents had organized a war to capture the Throne of God, because they erroneously believed that the life force was housed in the Throne itself.[1] They reasoned … if they could secure the position or the Throne of God, they would have power over the hidden secret of the life force. Yet, when they had unplugged, it had done something to their memory so they had forgotten that the source of the life force was not in the chair, but rather in and from only One Source and One Spirit of Life—God Himself. This was a big mistake! The secret of the life force was derived from the undisclosed combination of wisdom and love. So not only was it in God, but there were absolutely no other sources of wisdom and love in all of the Universe. How wrong can one get! The secret to eternal youth was not in a position of power. The throne of power should never have been LUCIFER'S goal because the power did not give you the life force—the life force gave you power, and you cannot buy the life force, for it is solely in God and only given by God to a Created being with conditions. And why fight against God? It was like a desk computer stabbing at the Mainframe Computer. If you kill the Mainframe, you end your life too. Absurd! But blinded and now desperately thirsty for this living water[2]—since the pipelines had been cut off—they waged this impossible war and lost. It was a victory for the Heavens, for the blinding, deadly pride was expelled. Had it remained, it would have eventually diffused mortality to every created being, causing much devastation to the Kingdom. The Heavens rejoiced as all the awkward, uncomfortable, angry, wicked spirits departed. Freedom and love remained, as *the strong Connections* to *The Source* endured in the Angels who

---

1   Psalm 47:8
2   Jeremiah 17:13, John 7:38

It was a victory for the Heavens, for the blinding, deadly pride was expelled. Had it remained, it would have eventually diffused mortality to every created being, causing much devastation to the Kingdom.

were left behind.

From the stars to the Earth, pride was not eradicated but rather transferred… and now woe to the Earth![1] This deadly virus called pride smashed into the Earth like a meteorite. Once this GREAT DRAGON, LUCIFER, got to his feet and climbed from the pit, he rose back up with his fist and face to the Heavens and spewed threats… that if he had enough time and power, he could persuade beings that were more loosely connected to The Source to turn against the rule of God. SATAN implied that the first war was lost simply because God did not play fair. No matter what the accusation, The Source of All Wisdom—God Almighty—knew that all this noise from SATAN was completely unfounded, but He curiously allowed it.

THE CREATION OF MAN

Indeed, God took the challenge and created the Earth, and it was good.[2] And then He created another being called man. God created him in His own image and He said that it was very good and gave mankind freedom and dominion over the animals of the Earth.[3]

SATAN had made the accusation to God that the Angels were not free-willed agents. But how could that be? SATAN himself had made the choice to disconnect from The Source, not to mention all of his demonic followers. So both Angels and mankind were given free will. But man was made differently—he was created to be lower than the Angels[4] and more vulnerable than the Angels. This vulnerability difference was somewhat due to the makeup of

1   Revelation 12:12
2   Genesis 1:12
3   Genesis 1:26-27
4   Hebrews 2:6-8

his spiritual senses. Even though man's ears could hear the leading of God, he was allowed the whispers of demons all of his life if he so chose because SATAN would never be dispelled on Earth. But most of the weakness difference would be due to the environment that they would be put in. Earth was a temporary testing ground and a place where God would allow both Angels and demons to coexist. This coexistence of good and evil could voice either TRUTH or lies in the ears, but what was heard could be controlled by the listener. Like a radio, man could turn either voice on or off. It was a dangerous experiment, because the mind of mankind could become so confused in the process that they go insane.[1] Nevertheless, The Great CEO set up this advantage because of the taunts of SATAN.

So God made man and placed them in a paradise that resembled parts of the Heavens, and He called it the Garden of Eden. And God allowed the ANCIENT SERPENT to freely roam the Garden. Why would God bother with such a challenge since He knew that SATAN was still blinded by his pride and that his accusations were unfounded? It is because God was going to use the challenge for the soul—as a sieve to divide good from evil. And in the end, the wheat would be separated from the chaff, the sheep from the goats.[2] In addition, He would use Earth as a training ground for eternity, for the Saints would one day judge the world. The Apostle called Paul wisely said, *"Do you not know that the saints will judge the world? And if you are to judge the world, are you not competent to judge trivial cases? Do you not know that we will judge angels? How much more the things of this life!"*[3]

---

1   Mark 5:1-20
2   Matthew 3:12, Matthew 25:32
3   I Corinthians 6:2-3

THE INCUBATOR OF APPRECIATION

The gift of shared life with man in His own image was an incredibly generous, expensive, incomprehensible gift. With only casual observation, man could easily see the great chasm of genius and position between man and God. And Eden was an incredible environment for being able to use all the senses to view God's handiwork—ranging from a variety of species, botany, and provisions. When man was created and his eyes opened, God made sure that it was an environment full to the brim of His incomparable artistical handiwork… Amazing![1] It was everything that described the genius of God's endless creativity and His boundless love. Not only were there millions of created items, but God made each created substance too complex to research and comprehend in one lifetime, thus generating appreciation and delight from birth to eternity that was inexcusable not to have.

An example of this is the multifaceted human eye, which has microscopic rod and cone cells made to absorb light waves that in turn stimulate the nerve endings connected to the brain cells, which then produce an image in the mind—impulses interpreting color, shape, details, and distance. Obviously incomprehensible. Total comprehension means that you could duplicate the human eye, but after 3,000 years of accumulated studies, mankind would be doing well to unravel just some of the facts about vision. Just this one topic is a fantastical, intriguing experience, besides being a generous gift to mankind. In other words, clearly a human could never see, touch, or experience in one lifetime—or even in eternity—all that God had created on Earth, thus alleviating the concept of boredom and creating everlasting fascination, intrigue, and therefore gratitude and

---

1   *Genesis 2:8-14*

In other words, clearly a human could never see, touch, or experience in one lifetime—or even in eternity—all that God had created on Earth, thus alleviating the concept of boredom and creating everlasting fascination, intrigue, and therefore gratitude and indebtedness. Indeed, the Garden of Eden was the incubator of appreciation.

indebtedness. Indeed, the Garden of Eden was the incubator of appreciation.

This experience, as in Heaven, was set up on purpose to create a chain reaction … from appreciation to love, from love to a complete connection, from a connection to eternal life. The end result would create a world of worship so that the Kingdom of God would come on Earth as it was in Heaven.[1]

It was all about a relationship with God. The Genius of All Geniuses did not just make man in His own image, but sought after *a bond*—the spirit of man to the Spirit of God. It was His good

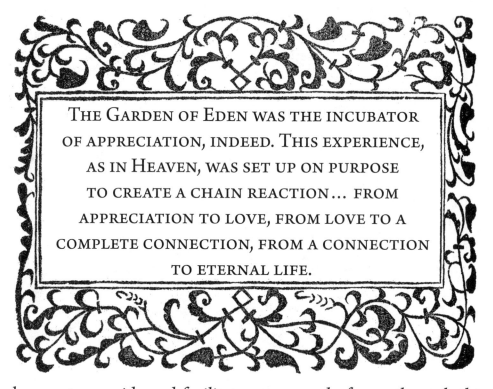

THE GARDEN OF EDEN WAS THE INCUBATOR OF APPRECIATION, INDEED. THIS EXPERIENCE, AS IN HEAVEN, WAS SET UP ON PURPOSE TO CREATE A CHAIN REACTION… FROM APPRECIATION TO LOVE, FROM LOVE TO A COMPLETE CONNECTION, FROM A CONNECTION TO ETERNAL LIFE.

pleasure to provide and facilitate every need of man through this bond. On top of that, for sheer joy, He programmed a microchip of His genius into the mind of man so that he could become skillful and productive, and in his own way, consider himself semi-creative. God's joy was much like that of a father passing down his skill to his son. God was so full of love and genius that it was His delight to direct all of creation—from the smallest microorganism to the largest creature walking or swimming the Earth. *This Connection* to God and access to His ingenious, wise, creative, joyous, and brilliant

1   *Matthew 6:10*

Spirit was priceless—like a wireless or live Wi-Fi or internet link to 𝕿𝖍𝖊 𝕲𝖗𝖊𝖆𝖙 𝕴 𝕬𝖒. Simply mind-boggling—being able to access the Heavenly Search Engine. This opportunity for man to link to 𝕿𝖍𝖊 𝕾𝖔𝖚𝖗𝖈𝖊 𝖔𝖋 𝖂𝖎𝖘𝖉𝖔𝖒 𝖆𝖓𝖉 𝕷𝖔𝖛𝖊 was so over-the-top generous that one could hardly think about it without shouting for joy. And the feeling that you have when you are connected is like the feeling you have when a child climbs up in your lap and puts their head on your chest and snuggles with you. This love is warm and it is beautiful. The temptation for man was "the source temptation"—for once connected, without appreciation, some would want to believe that they were the source.

SATAN'S NEW WAR STRATEGY

In Heaven, LUCIFER'S rebellion was overt—he was open and clear about his intentions. Yet after having lost the first straightforward rebellion in Heaven, LUCIFER and his demons regrouped and formed a new covert war strategy—deceit—and refined his weapons, the lies.[1] Again, the difference between Earth and Heaven was that the TRUTH was allowed to co-mingle with lies, something that had never happened in Heaven where only TRUE RELIGION reigned. Using this "lie and truth coexistence," the rebellion would never look like rebellion again—and that was THE GREAT DECEIT.[2]

The angry eyes of all demons were hidden behind a wicked smile, and as with all poisonous snakes, the ANCIENT SERPENT had a split or forked tongue. There was a purpose in the split tongue: one side of the tongue would express TRUTH and then the other side would express the lie, thus confusing the TRUTH. A conjunction is always

1 Romans 3:13
2 II Thessalonians 2

used with this half-truth. For example, SATAN might say, "You need to obey God... *BUT*... God knows you are only human." What is *that* supposed to mean? All humans had the same *Employee Manual* which said to stay connected to the will of God or you will die. This forked tongue would facilitate a new type of deceit that was even more insidious than could be imagined, where man—unlike the Angels—would have absolutely no idea that disobedience would cause them to be disconnected from their precious God or life source. It was a form of sweet-looking pride. Those who listened to the TRUTH mixed with the lies would have no idea that God was no longer favoring them. While in the pit, SATAN had time to scheme a POWERFUL DELUSION that would cause man to unknowingly exalt himself. It was the deceit of deceits whispered in the ears of man, where mankind would not believe that they were not the apple of God's eye if you told them.

There was a purpose in the split tongue: one side of the tongue would express Truth and then the other side would express the lie, thus confusing the Truth.

THE OTHER GROUND RULES FOR EARTH

Simply put, with the power of deceit, SATAN was strengthening his false religion that was a copycat of Heaven, Incorporated—being

To be on guard would be the essential protection for the soul, which was indeed a prize to be won! So just as God had His secret power for life, Satan and his demons had a secret power for lawlessness and death—but both were a choice.

allowed to use counterfeit miracles, signs, and wonders.[1] Unfortunately, this delusion would be so powerful that it would cause an ABOMINATION THAT WOULD LEAD TO DESOLATION,[2] where man would oppose and exalt himself over everything that is called God or is worshipped, so that he sets himself up in God's temple, proclaiming himself to be God.[3]

But knowing all this, The Heavenly Father, who has all pow-

---

1   II Thessalonians 2:9

2   Daniel 9:27, Daniel 11:31, Matthew 24:15, Mark 13:14

3   II Thessalonians 2:4

er, Amen, allowed SATAN'S new war strategy to be introduced on Earth to the free-will agents but with a time limit—a sort of stop clock—and it was called mortality and each would face a Judgment Day.[1] That should have spoken loud and clear to mankind that "God Rules!" but somehow SATAN would trump this TRUTH and convince man that they were all saved. While SATAN'S goal was revenge, God used this timed race as a 70 to 90-year job interview—a sieve to reveal good and bad hearts.

So by the end of one term of life, man was given ample time to see if he adored or despised God, using the barometer of obedience. You would obey whom you loved.[2] If you were connected and followed the Guiding Hand (obedience), you loved God; if you followed your own desires or SATAN, you loved SATAN.

In addition, God, Who was in control, would allow this war strategy to be used as a training ground for the Elect. The Elect were those who had made the choice to obey God, thus their obedience was easy, delightful, and welcomed. These tests from SATAN would teach the Saints spiritual combat.

Now, the basic rules and the *Holy Manual* remained the same on Earth as it was in Heaven. The *Holy Scriptures* explained that the path to eternal life was a *Connection* to The Source of the Universe. It was clear from the beginning that staying connected to God gives eternal life and disconnecting from God is the path to death. Dialogue with God was essential—a word that would later be called prayer. Those connected would understand the value of constant interchange. It was also clear that *Connection* and authority were synonymous, for many times *the Spirit* was given through the authorities above you. Obedience was the fruit of a

1   *Genesis 6:3*
2   *John 14:15, I John 3:24*

40

In this battle of the ages, the difference between Earth and Heaven was that the Truth was allowed to co-mingle with lies. Where the Truth would regenerate life, the lie would murder.

good connection and the path to purifying *the Connection*, making sure there were no blocks or occlusions. Again, disruptions to *the Connection* were just like in the Heavens—idols or other loves before God could completely sever a connection.[1] TRUTH and love for God strengthened *the Connection*. It was clear in the *Holy Manual* that God alone was everything.

So just as God had His secret power for life, SATAN and his de-

---

1   *Exodus 20*

mons had a secret power for lawlessness and death—but both were a choice.[1] What man did not know yet is that *the Connection* to God was everything and they needed to seek out and protect this interchange above all things![2] They needed to protect this pipeline at all costs, for man would learn that any obstruction to the lungs would block the essential breath of life and completely suffocate them... a horrible death. Choking on pride or lust would completely block the breath of life to the lungs. To be on guard would be the essential protection for the soul, which was indeed a prize to be won!

WITH THE GROUND RULES IN PLACE...

With this *Holy Manual* and the Garden of Eden as the backdrop, the stage and the ground rules of this Cosmic Challenge were set. The Garden of Eden was the environment to promote humility with a love for authority. The ANCIENT SERPENT was given permission to promote pride and the concept that the one under authority knows best. The Garden of Eden was an incubator of appreciation for God, but SATAN was present, ready to whisper the lie and promote the antithesis of appreciation... man merits, man deserves, man deserves a break from this connection every once in a while. Where the TRUTH would regenerate life, the lie would murder. In the ground rules, righteous Angels were sent to Earth to hover over each man, woman, and child, while assassins and murderers were allowed to disguise themselves and lurk nearby. So, with the stars set in place and the Earth spinning, the terrestrial time clock began, and round two of the Battle of the Ages was about to begin. ❧

---

1   II Thessalonians 2:7
2   Ephesians 6:18, Philippians 4:6

Righteous Angels were sent to Earth to hover over each man, woman, and child, while assassins and murderers were allowed to disguise themselves and lurk nearby.

Then one dark day, after much time of love and freedom and innocent days of enjoying the beautiful days in Paradise, an unexpected turn of events happened. The fiendish, blindsided attack was quick, sure, and devastating. Lucifer knew that timing and speed—creating an element of surprise—was everything.

44

The First Attack on Man

CHAPTER 3

Now remember, Paradise was the environment to promote humility with a love for authority. After God had planted a garden in the east in Eden, He put the man there who He had formed to work it and take care of it. The Creator made all kinds of trees grow out of the ground—trees that were pleasing to the eye and good for food. However, in the middle of the Garden was the tree of life and the knowledge of good and evil.[1] And then God commanded Adam… "You are free to eat from any tree in the garden; but you must not eat from the tree of the knowledge of good and evil, for when you eat of it you will surely die."[2]

---

1   *Genesis 2:8-9*
2   *Genesis 2:16-17*

ONE DARK DAY

Then one dark day, after much time of love and freedom and innocent days of enjoying the beautiful days in Paradise, an unexpected turn of events happened. Perhaps on this particular day the sun was darkened by the clouds and the brilliance of God in the Garden was dimmed. There is no record of all the circumstances—nevertheless, no one could argue that there was something different in the air, and it all materialized so fast that everyone wondered what had transpired, like the great calm before a tornado that descends on its victims in the night out of nowhere. Indeed, to this day few to none have been given the deepest insights into the details of this murderous attempt, save one… LUCIFER. The fiendish, blindsided attack was quick, sure, and devastating. How, when, where, and why? Saints are in such need to study all wars and their cause, their enemies, and their strategies—things that are absolutely essential so that battles and wars could or would never be initiated or lost again. In other words, the history of the "Garden Attack" should be one of the most researched events in history, but to date, it has been rarely discussed or recounted.

Society either believes that SATAN does not exist or that he plays more of a minor role than he does. But after all, is that not the foundation of THE GREAT DELUSION… to make the world believe that God is not at war with SATAN… that there are no demonic rulers, authorities, or powers of the dark world, nor spiritual forces of evil in the Heavenly realms?[1] Most have fallen asleep and see no reason to put on the battle armor, much less keep it on—for they believe there is no war for the soul of man, and the voices and lies are just a figment of the imagination.

---

1   *Ephesians 6:12*

THE DISGUISE OF SATAN

But I can testify that SATAN is real, and in the ground rules of this great contest, God allowed demons their request to be able to present themselves in a disguise as an Angel or the right to enter humans. It was SATAN'S idea to pose as a concerned friend or even a family member. SATAN trained the demons to speak lies in a soft, concerned voice. The greatest veiled skill of all was their incredible ability to invoke victimization faster than any being in the Universe.

Even though SATAN had other powers and counterfeit miracles up his sleeve, SATAN'S major weapon on this dark day was "the lie." The lie seems harmless, but it would prove to be more deadly to man than poison, cancer, or the atomic bomb. If people had only known from creation the power of twisted words, they would have fled the scene, closed their ears, and shut out the whispers.

After years of leading insurrections in the Heavens, LUCIFER learned from his past mistakes to never label sin as sin, defiance as defiance, rebellion as rebellion. Label these things as reasonable and expected solutions to your plight—expected behavior from weak mankind. SATAN'S new covert strategy was so hidden and undercover that it seemed like nothing—

just shop talk, the ramblings of a nobody. In complete disguise and under the nose of man, LUCIFER was able to hang out and chit-chat with words that were deadly.

LUCIFER knew that timing and speed—creating an element of surprise—was everything. He had learned to wait for just the right moment and stay still behind the scenes like a spider in Eden for so long that Adam and Eve suspected nothing. Then his murderous spirit and fatal lies would descend on the head of the man and the woman like a guillotine. The bite of the fangs would be lightning fast, and like all venom, it would paralyze reason—moving quickly and filling the mind so that there was no chance of recovery.

SATAN had planned and schemed this day for years… So the AN-CIENT DRAGON who breathed fire went about the Garden as an innocent snake, one of the faithful subjects, waiting patiently for just the right moment to strike mankind with his venom.[1] His timing was impeccable. This was the day. It seemed like any other day to Adam and Eve, so SATAN—without contest—crept near. I can assure you that what was about to transpire was no accident.

> Now the serpent was more crafty than any of the wild animals the LORD God had made. He said to the woman, "Did God really say, 'You must not eat from any tree in the garden'?" The woman said to the serpent, "We may eat fruit from the trees in the garden, but God did say, 'You must not eat fruit from the tree that is in the middle of the garden, and you must not touch it, or you will die.'" "You will not surely die," the serpent said to the woman. "For God knows that when you eat of it your eyes will be opened, and you will be like God, knowing good and evil." When the woman saw that the fruit of the tree was good for food and pleasing to the eye,

---

1   Matthew 12:34

and also desirable for gaining wisdom, she took some and ate it. She also gave some to her husband, who was with her, and he ate it. Then the eyes of both of them were opened, and they realized they were naked; so they sewed fig leaves together and made coverings for themselves. Then the man and his wife heard the sound of the LORD God as he was walking in the garden in the cool of the day, and they hid from the LORD God among the trees of the garden. But the LORD God called to the man, "Where are you?" He answered, "I heard you in the garden, and I was afraid because I was naked; so I hid." And he said, "Who told you that you were naked? Have you eaten from the tree that I commanded you not to eat from?" The man said, "The woman you put here with me— she gave me some fruit from the tree, and I ate it."

Then the LORD God said to the woman, "What is this you have done?" The woman said, "The serpent deceived me, and I ate." (Genesis 3:1-13)

THE GARDEN LIES EXPOSED

What Adam and Eve did may seem like a misdemeanor to you, however, this was an enormous, atrocious loss for the Heavens and a dreadful direction for mankind. Sin entered the Earth for the first time on this very dark day like an unexpected tornado and changed the landscape forever.

How is this possible? Adam and Eve were uneducated to the real intent of SATAN. People perish every day from the simple lack of knowledge.[1] They were caught off guard. Let me paint you a candid and reliable picture. "More crafty than the other animals" was an

---

1   *Hosea 4:6*

Satan quietly and patiently spins a sticky web and then at just the right moment assaults and paralyzes the victim and then continues to wrap the web of lies.

understatement. When ꙅᴀᴛᴀɴ is unmasked, he is seen for what he is… a poisonous viper, with fangs full of deadly venom that, if allowed to absorb into one's bloodstream, would most certainly bring pain, death, and demise. The shrouded ꙅᴀᴛᴀɴ presented himself as sweet and concerned, but in reality he is more like a large, ugly spider who quietly and patiently spins a sticky web and then at just the right moment assaults and paralyzes the victim and then continues to wrap the web of lies around the victim until he unresistingly allows the devil's fangs to suck the blood. All reality visions are grotesque, and yet all demons were given the right to disguise themselves so that they can get close to their prey.

THE WEAPON—THE LIE

Do not be deceived by looks, neither be deceived by his weapon…the lie. Look again… this lie is a weapon that is more like a razor blade or scissors, that when listened to can immediately cut the cords of a parachute to God, allowing a free fall to one's death.

Now, when you break this passage down, you find five paralyzing venom bites with a sticky web to secure its victim—resulting in five razor-sharp lies to cut the arteries to the *life force.*

Lie number one… "Did God really say, 'You must not eat from any tree in the garden,' you poor thing?" This is the victim lie that always comes first, and this victim lie opens up the door for the other four lies—but if avoided, closes the door for the other four lies. Since it is so strategic, let us thoroughly examine this first victimization lie.

How does it work? It uses any words that move man's eyes off of what he has and onto what he does not have… the power of the lie that "you deserve more."

Yet, how preposterous! The generous God and Spoiler of the Universe created man, his mouth, his taste buds, and the different flavors for man—for sheer enjoyment. God was not saving the best food for Himself. This was not for God. And then God gave man hundreds—perhaps thousands—of different food sources and asks man not to eat one. Please!

At least Eve addressed the first lie and said, "We MAY eat fruit from the trees in the garden, but God did say, 'You must not eat fruit from the tree that is in the middle of the garden, and you must not touch it, or you will die.'"[1] But apparently some of the victim venom had already entered her system, or otherwise she would have said...

"I dare you to insult an extremely generous God who has given us the best menu. There are not multiple restrictions, limitations, and constraints—there is one tiny restraint, narrowed down to one tiny location in a paradise. God has spoiled us and no one could consider anything God does as a limitation at all, but rather protection! SATAN, be gone."

A strong defense of God runs snakes away. But Eve and Adam had a weak answer, for when the first lie entered the ears of the listener, it had the ability to peak their curiosity and give the insinuation that they were missing something—so they kept listening, which in turn twisted their appreciation into expectation, which

---

1   *Genesis 3:2-3*

meant that they were open to the distorting lie that man was not blessed but rather was a victim.

Oh, the danger of the first lie—words that have the sway to make man feel cheated, or that others to have it better, etc. The poison deadens the senses and even on just the first words it starts to paralyze the reason. Look how quickly the lies of SATAN can reduce the most generous God into a tight-fisted, stingy God and reduce a blessed person into a needy person—from grateful to greedy, just like that.

The implications: "Did God really impose a restriction on you? You deserve more. Are you even sure that you interpreted that law the right way? You work hard—you deserve an indulgence. These rules do not apply to you." These falsehoods can make the richest person in the world want more money and the most obese person in the world believe he should eat more food. Adam and Eve never saw the sticky web or the fangs. However, they did notice the water that was dripping out of their eyes—what was this? Prior to the rebellion, no one had seen or heard of tears in Heaven, for no one knew how to feel sorry for themselves. With a focus on the TRUTH of how much you had been given, there was no agony. But now with just the thought of what they were missing and what they deserved, they felt pain and wept for their own pitiful plight.

Yes, God had made a rule for man, but boundaries are precious railings or balustrades to keep mankind from falling off the cliff. Adam and Eve never visualized SATAN removing the protective rail and pushing them off the precipice.

Boundaries have a secondary use—when presented with the lies, they test the heart of man. Adam and Eve were being tested. Was this a hard test for man? I would say this was a challenging job for SATAN—to make a surplus look like depravity. The power of turning "too much" into "too little"—to make man feel like he needs more, more, more. This can only be accomplished through people who have their eyes closed to reality and lustfully open to more—they may be surrounded by too much, but they crave what others have or the one thing they do not have. Some people have many friends, and yet they focus on the one person who does not like them. God was clear in His Manual: do not covet what someone else has.[1] God had sent His powerful, protective Angels, and they whispered the TRUTH—but Adam and Eve turned the Heavenly stream of TRUTH off and turned the volume of SATAN up. Nev-

---

1   *Exodus 20:17*

er forget that without the first bite from SATAN, you could resist the rest. It was the first victimization lie that even sanctioned the next four spider bites.

Lie number two... "You will not surely die."[1] One would think that this is a harder lie to accept. Even though Adam and Eve had not seen anyone die or been able to prove the connection between disobedience and curses and death, it is surprising how little resistance that Adam and Eve gave this lie, for they had heard with their own ears from the mouth of God, *"You must not eat fruit from the tree that is in the middle of the garden, and you must not touch it, or you will die."*[2]

It seems that if direct defiance is not immediately corrected or punished, the wicked irrationally believe, like SATAN, that death is just a false threat. Delayed punishment gives false security, but have no doubt: if you touch the tree, you will die, for it cuts the electrical cord to The Source of All Electricity, unplugs the terminal from The Mainframe Computer, and blocks the sap from The Vine to the branches.

SATAN implied, "That does not even sound like the loving God we know. What God really expects is for you to eat that fruit." What SATAN is planting in lie number one is that the commands are too difficult to achieve, therefore the punishment does not fit the crime. What he is saying is that these commands are lofty goals and therefore are unreachable, so they are simply superfluous suggestions. Since you believe lie number one is true, it follows that you believe you are not going to die from eating this fruit.

Now a third injection of venom... innocent sounding lie number three... *"For God knows that when you eat of it your eyes will be*

---

1   Genesis 3:4
2   Genesis 2:16-17

opened."[1] Who is not tempted to have better vision? Satan was implying that they would see more of the big picture. Lies one, two, and three planted seeds of suggestions—from feeling sorry to "I deserve more," then "God knows you will be okay if you indulge—in fact, more experienced."

It is true that they saw more, but it was not of the world—it was their own nakedness and vulnerability. Indeed, all of the Heavens knew that you become blinded when you touch the fruit of pride. The Angels were there to warn, but the Heavenly radio was turned down and the radio from Hades was turned up—besides the fact that the venom was continuing to paralyze the senses. Just listen-

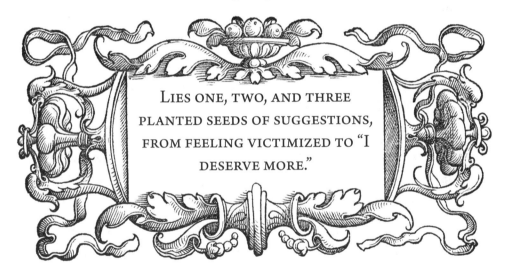

LIES ONE, TWO, AND THREE PLANTED SEEDS OF SUGGESTIONS, FROM FEELING VICTIMIZED TO "I DESERVE MORE."

ing was blinding Adam and Eve to the Truth. Satan had turned the safety rail into an unnecessary, condescending command from the Heavens. He was putting mankind in danger's way. The Liar convinced man that wrath is non-existent. Satan introduced "expected disobedience"—once favored, always favored—in fact... once born—eternal favor.

---

1   *Genesis 3:5*

All the vulnerability weaknesses of man mixed with this one speck of pride creates this one moment—a moment in time that you forget that you cannot even stand up without the help of God ... a mental block to the beauty of the environment, the value of life, and the joy of *the Connection*. It seems impossible for SATAN to do this, but with the first three lies... snip, snip, snip—the scissors have cut some of the major ropes of this parachute to God, all in less than a minute of time. But Adam and Eve kept listening.

Now lie number four… *"For God knows that when you eat of it your eyes will be opened, and you will be like God, knowing good and evil."*[1]

The Pandora's box that was opened filled the Earth with a swarm of confusion, and it birthed the sin, "You know. You will know what to do on your own. You do not have to use God's Spirit to guide you into what and how much to eat or drink or buy or talk or anything. God put you on Earth and expects you to make decisions on your own. You know—you know what is best for you." There was something about this lie that could make the barnacle on the side of a ship believe that it could not only detach from the side of the ship and live, but also then be able to steer the ship. Overconfidence takes regular people and turns them into fools.

Adam and Eve bought into the implication that God had knowingly been holding out on useful and valuable mysteries. But the TRUTH was that God had given them knowledge and self-esteem. The "tree of the knowledge of good and evil" was not a source—it could not give Adam and Eve open eyes or knowledge. The tree gave God information about the heart of man, whether man was good or evil. There is a big difference. God had never cheated man—SATAN was the one robbing them. Indeed, Adam and Eve were not more knowledgeable after eating the fruit—they were more confused and

---

1   *Genesis 3:5*

56

insecure—hiding behind fig leaves, less in the image of God. SATAN completely falsely accused God and lied about the purpose of the tree. It was the opposite—when they ate the forbidden fruit, it gave God knowledge about their hearts. They were too ready to believe the worst of God and too anxious to have His position. You want to be more like God? Then I have a tip for you… desire the characteristics of God—not His position, not His power, not His throne. Adam and Eve were becoming greedy—more like LUCIFER and less like God.

Lie number five... Moving quickly to the fourth sentence from LUCIFER and the fifth lie… It says, "The woman saw that the fruit of the tree was good for food and pleasing to the eye, and also desirable for gaining wisdom."[1] The first four lies say that you have misunderstood the commands, and lie number five is the icing on the cake, which says, "Not only have you misjudged and believed God that it was detrimental to eat that fruit—the fruit is superior. You will be even better off—you will be wiser." The final injection of the fangs of SATAN—that human desire is expected, good, pleasing, and beneficial. In four short sentences, SATAN turned great good into suspected evil and great evil into a good idea— THE GREAT DELUSION. For this split moment in time, Adam and Eve supposed they should and could be their own gods with their own wisdom, and that is called greed—and they desired something on Earth above God, and that is called idolatry. When the final poison entered, mankind did the unthinkable—they took some of the fruit and ate it, Eve first and then Adam. How deceived can you get?—for this had been the only restriction in Paradise.

---

1   *Genesis 3:6*

The final injection of the fangs of Satan—that human desire is expected, good, pleasing, and beneficial. In four short sentences, Satan turned great good into suspected evil and great evil into a good idea— the Great Delusion. Mankind did the unthinkable—they took some of the fruit and ate it, Eve first and then Adam.

THE POWER OF FIVE LIES

To summarize these five lies... The combination of "Did God really say you could not have anything to eat, you poor thing? You need more," and "You will not surely die if you help yourself" are by far the deadliest weapon of destruction against mankind and has claimed more lives than all physical wars put together throughout history. How dreadful is this deceit.

What SATAN had set up was a series of words that were not so blatantly obvious against God that Adam and Eve would run away. SATAN skillfully leads the listeners down the path of feeling sorry for themselves, then feeling needy, and then to a God-approved solution of taking care of their "needs" by becoming their own bosses or gods—becoming like God, ruling themselves. Man did not notice the forked tongue. Man was not aware that they were insulting God and defying God, and they moved too quickly to put enough thought into their actions at all—that is why it is a called a trick or delusion. You believe you are okay and are doing what is right while you are actually doing something that is robbing and ruining your life!

OPPOSITE WORLD

From lie or bite number one—"Poor you, you do not have enough, you need more, more, more—more food, more wisdom, more of a vision"—to lie number two... "If you take care of yourself, you will not die,"—and lies number three, four, and five... "You know you would be more godly and have more wisdom if you would just make decisions on your own"—LUCIFER led them to THE GREAT DIS-CONNECTION... that they would be better off if they looked out for themselves, and since God was not providing for them, they needed to provide for themselves and they really needed to watch out because God was just using them to work His Garden. By simply using lies, SATAN reversed the authority line and made God out to be the needy, wanting one in this relationship, rather than man being needy. The definition of a parasite is an organism that lives in or on another organism (its host) and benefits by deriving nutrients at the host's expense. The lies make God the parasite and man the source, but God is The Host. He is The Host and The Life Source, and man is the needy, life-sucking parasite attached to poor God, like a fetus in utero who demands the best of what the host eats. Life force connections only drain God and give life to man. Obedience never helps the authority—it gives life to the one under authority. It is opposite world.

So what happened? Let us face it, none of what SATAN promised materialized. Eve did her first shopping on her own and wound up in deep trouble. When Adam and Eve ate the fruit, it opened up their eyes all right—not to wisdom, but to who they were—and for the first time, they saw that they were naked with unpresentable parts. They were not gods after all. SATAN'S mask was removed, and as it turns out, he is the blood-sucking vampire. Have you ever wondered why SATAN wants you so badly? It is pure projection—he is disconnected and he needs you to work his demonic garden. He wants to use you like a battery since he is not a source. He uses you and he wants you to disconnect from God, and when you are all the way dead, stuck in his web of words, he feeds on your blood. So his lies promise you life and give you death—it is a trap. God promises life and gives abundant life and eternity and much, much more—it is an opportunity!

Five toxic lies made man feel confident and reversed the position

None of what Satan promised materialized. So his lies promise you life and give you death.

of 𝔗𝔥𝔢 𝔥𝔬𝔰𝔱 and the parasite, without fearing the wrath of 𝔗𝔥𝔢 𝔥𝔬𝔰𝔱! What a disguise—what a sticky, luring web of lies—what a venom so powerful to take man and turn him on his 𝔠𝔯𝔢𝔞𝔱𝔬𝔯, take a child and have him turn on the parent, take an employee and have him turn on his employer, take a barnacle on the side of the ship and tell him he will live if he detaches. Mankind should flee the lies.

THE RESPONSIBILITY OF MAN

Nevertheless, as formidable as the Spiritual Warfare was, the responsibility was still man's, for 𝔊𝔬𝔡 did not ask about SATAN. 𝔊𝔬𝔡 asked, "What is this you have done? You have attacked My Sovereignty. You have thrown a relationship with me away and chosen a relationship with LUCIFER?" Man must slow down and hear God speaking to each of us. "What have we done?" It is all about personal responsibility.

Man was without excuse… for the TRUTH is that man will never be a good guide, nor ever a source of wisdom, and God cannot surrender His Supremacy or Sovereignty, unless He wants all created beings to be cut off from the Only Source of Life.

Adam and Eve had some excuse… they were uninformed about the real image of SATAN and the deadly nature of the lie. I do not apologize for repeating myself concerning the real image of The SERPENT and his weapons and war tactics, because these essential facts do not seem to sink in. Over the centuries, The DRAGON's lethal approach remains cloaked, for it is obvious that much of mankind remains uninformed, unaware, and unconcerned about the lies and the SATANIC false preachers. There is no fear, for the Church has never prepared for Spiritual Warfare enough—nor have they banned these lies from the tongue, the household, the society, or the congregation. Perhaps now mankind will take more notice and learn to use their spiritual antennas to detect the presence of SATAN and his demons.

So how deadly are these lies? In just four sentences or forty-three words, the lies created THE GREAT DELUSION… that God is greedy and man is needy, undermining God and empowering man enough to defy The Lord of All and "play" god. Adam and Eve thought that this was just another day in Paradise, but they were isolated targets in an insidious war. So, at the end of this long, dark day, the prideful LUCIFER flaunted the victory sign high in the air to his cheering demons and confidently said, "Pay attention boys, this is how it is done." ❧

So, at the end of this long, dark day, the prideful Lucifer flaunted the victory sign high in the air to his cheering demons and confidently said, "Pay attention boys, this is how it is done."

If only humans were taught from birth the real picture of the insidious warfare—if only they could wake up and see that they are assigned a spiritual stalker, a murderous assassin, a demonic antagonist to their souls.

The Rescue

CHAPTER 4

So initially, rebellion to 𝔊𝔬𝔡 was unheard of in the Universe, and then through pride—which is also jealousy and hatred of authority—it was released in the pristine Heavens like dark, molten lava oozing out on a mountain of deep, white snow. LUCIFER in his prideful security had attacked the Sovereignty of 𝔊𝔬𝔡. This SERPENT successfully transferred this false security so that he disconnected quite a few angels from 𝕿𝖍𝖊 𝕾𝖔𝖚𝖗𝖈𝖊 𝖔𝖋 𝕷𝖔𝖛𝖊.

Once disengaged from the beautiful, white King—the feather-like wings that once glistened in the starlight withered into black, bat-like wings.

Therefore, these once powerful angels shriveled up into mentally ill, almost unrecognizably distorted creatures, full of projection and killer hate. Once disengaged from the beautiful, white King—the feather-like wings that once glistened in the starlight withered into black, bat-like wings.

But of course, the God who is LOVE would not allow this hate to abide in the Heavens of love. So He banished this false security called pride to the Earth. The firmaments were restored to being full of humble, joyful Angels who did not dare project, but stayed focused on The Creator and looking inward. Another way to say this is that the Angels returned to being personally responsible for their own behavior. They were insecure in a good way so that they considered personal introspection an essential function. Each Angel would go to great lengths to protect their own connection to The Source of Endless Life so that they could see all gorgeous and good things from the Heavens.

Notice that those who are self-confident and full of pride will not stop their incessant blaming. Anger is transferred from one person or situation to another. Pride cannot be wrong; TRUTH is wasted on arrogance. TRUTH will never penetrate the fortress of the prideful heart for even one second. The prideful are indignant at the suggestion that they need any counsel from an authority, for they fancy themselves as a source of information—as intellectuals with brilliant, superior religious philosophies. They fantasize that if God is upset with them, it is simply because He is jealous.

THE REVERSAL OF REALITY

So, as stated earlier, the one-time successful entrepreneur, LUCIFER, tried to reinstate his business in the Garden of Eden. To recruit employees, he infused the poison of fear, doubt of authority, and victimization, and proceeded to encourage man to disconnect from his Creator. So powerful was this GREAT DELUSION that in one sentence spoken with a forked tongue, a victim would sit and entertain three more lies. With exactly 43 words, THE GREAT DELUSION seemed for sure to be reality. In other words, SATAN made right look wrong and wrong look right. This DEMON could take all light and make man think that he sees dark. He could take all good and have men believe they see evil, make generous look stingy, and make freedom look like slavery and slavery look like freedom. SATAN took *the Connection* of authority and made it a suspicious and repulsive thing—for "the subordinate really knows what is best." Do you not see all this as freaky? These lies have been left so unrestrained that today, instead of being frightened of antiauthority, you are frightened of authority—and morality is immorality and immorality is moral. This is the reversal of reality. This is the Reality Reversal, which is the death to Sovereignty. Instead of protecting this relationship at all costs, man throws it away. Man finds authority irritating and avoids rather than seeks its presence and dishonors rather than honors it. This is ignorance! If only each man, woman, and child knew that authority was a saving communication link to the Heavens, they would strive to hear and see and obey *this authority Connection* direction.

Now, after centuries of this, the Reality Reversal is almost complete so that antiauthority is natural. The inanimate, such as the trees, are now said to be wiser than all of mankind (such as in the movies "Avatar" and "Pocahontas"). The animals are all smarter than the children in every movie, but this started before Disney with a movie called "Lassie." Notice that in almost every movie, the younger are always smarter than the adults, such as in the movie "The Little Mermaid." The youth are smarter than their teachers, the wives are smarter than their husbands, the employees are smarter than their bosses, and citizens are smarter than the governing authorities. $\mathfrak{SA}$-$\mathfrak{TAN'S}$ lies make it healthy to disengage from authority.

The TRUTH is the exact opposite of the lie—for example, $\mathfrak{SATAN}$ teaches you (as a child) that wisdom/good guidance will most often originate with you, but the reality is that most commonly $\mathfrak{God}$ sends His wisdom and guidance through the authorities above you. When you mock the voice above you, you unknowingly cut the line to $\mathfrak{God\ Himself}$—so, essential communication, provisions, and blessings are cut off. In the future, the antiauthority lie will be strengthened and it will become more dreadful, as hate will rule and the love of most will grow cold[1] so that we will witness even more murder and false accusations and putting parents in jail. The essential nature of authority and how the authority line is the essential lifeline to salvation has been suspiciously ignored, and if we do not wake up and realize its place in the salvation of mankind—mankind will destroy themselves.

If only humans were taught from birth the real picture of the insidious warfare—if only they could wake up and see that they are assigned a spiritual stalker, a murderous assassin, a demonic antagonist to their souls—they would be more equipped with the Helmet of Salvation, the Belt of Truth, and the Shield of Faith.[2] They would rush to a True Church—a safe haven from demons—the rare place that teaches defense and survival classes. After centuries of work, $\mathfrak{SATAN}$ has managed to create such a comfortable delusion that Saints do not fear leaving their spiritual armor in the closet every day. Religious seekers, as a rule, never get past just gathering a few religious facts, and have no clue they are in a spiritual war sur-

---

1   Matthew 24:12
2   Ephesians 6

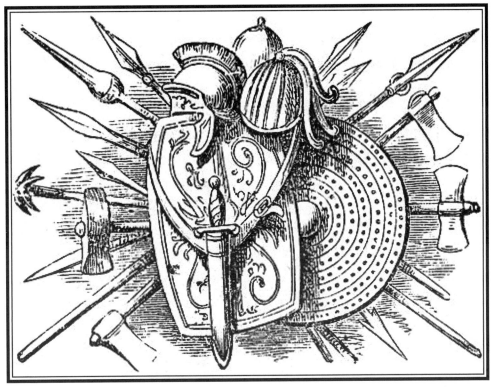

Stand firm then, with the belt of truth buckled around your waist, with the breastplate of righteousness in place, and with your feet fitted with the readiness that comes from the gospel of peace. In addition to all this, take up the shield of faith, with which you can extinguish all the flaming arrows of the evil one. Take the helmet of salvation and the sword of the Spirit, which is the word of God. And pray in the Spirit on all occasions with all kinds of prayers and requests.
(Ephesians 6:14-18)

rounded by expert deceivers. LUCIFER lied. You are not okay and you are not better off. You are surrounded by lies; only listening to TRUTH will set you free. Do you want the TRUTH? Well, it is probably 180 degrees away from what you have been taught in this day and age.

For the few who are awake to the spiritual world, it is clear when people today have been bitten by the ANCIENT SERPENT, for just like the adverse alteration of the exquisite angels to dreadful demons, mankind experiences the same transformation so that they become hardly recognizable, depending upon the vice. Also, upon disconnecting from God and His True Church (for there are many false ones), they desperately grasp onto forbidden sins of which they were once prone. If they were prone to lust for food, they would rapidly regain their weight. If it was drugs or sexual lust, praise of man or whatever vice they were attracted to, they would dive into unrestrained dissipation. Why? Listen closely, for this is profound. It is because once you unplug, you find out you have no breath of life or Spirit of love and joy; you are so empty and depressed that you go after much more of what you were tempted with in the first place. Jesus said, *"When an evil spirit comes out of a man, it goes through arid places seeking rest and does not find it. Then it says, 'I will return to the house I left.' When it arrives, it finds the house unoccupied, swept clean and put in order. Then it goes and takes with it seven other spirits more wicked than itself, and they go in and live there. And the final condition of that man is worse than the first."* (Matthew 12:43-45)

So the prideful are worse than they were after they disconnected because they do not put their guard up—and the self-righteous do not return to home base, nor do they ask The Creator why a creature was offering the exact opposite counsel. Antiauthority gives man this eerie self-confidence that their noncompliance is an astute, God-approved, superior, almost expected move of the mature. Pride believes it is a sign of intelligence to listen to SATAN'S new religion—like the people of Athens[1] who were always open to the latest philosophy and discussing the latest entity to blame for the current woes of society. Pride is projection; egotism is confident that it does not need to change. Prideful superiority loves to give advice, dislikes taking advice, and hates to give credit. Adam and Eve should have sought God out and consulted the *Holy Manual*—

---

1   Acts 17

when they heard the exact opposite of what the Heavenly Father had said.

The victim lie that "your authority is too overbearing" is a deadly drink, but unfortunately it feels good going down and gives the victim a taste for more. The mixture of five lies creates a cocktail of numbing intoxication which results in "unknowing insolence" or "barely-aware defiance." The ANCIENT DRAGON is a flatterer who wants you to believe that "there is a whole world beyond the True Church and you are missing it—so go find it."

Most Saints have had no training by the false church leaders to detect the difference between The Spirit and the sensual.

How many children leave the True Church (for there are many false, hypocritical churches) and look for more? SATAN'S lies take the prodigal son[1] from a palace with feasts, servants, and respect, to a pigpen of starvation and disdain. The son leaves home convinced that there is more out there. For some, they never find their way back home. There is such a need to appreciate the opportunity of authority—*the Connection* to the life source.

THE BEGINNING OF SENSUAL DESIRE

It started with a choice of focus. The position of the eyes governs your connection. Adam and Eve had always had their eyes on The Creator, but for a moment in time, Adam and Eve saw that the fruit

---

1   *Luke 15:11-32*

was desirable. Now there are appropriate God-programmed desires that are led by the Spirit when you are plugged into The Heavenly Father. He created these pre-encoded desires to have a clear "on" and "off" switch. And it is true that a well-defined starting and stopping point can only be felt when connected to The Mainframe Computer—the Source of self-control. This Spirit that is placed is innate—so that infants know the exact kilocalorie the body needs each hour of the day (hunger and fullness). Thirst is an example of a feeling that is used to turn on drinking behavior, and satisfaction turns it off. This also applies to sleep, cleanliness, work, play, talking, working, etc. Once you find the Spirit from the Source, you can sense, feel, and know when you have a need and when you have had enough—where to go and what to be doing. It is a fantastical walk with God called a Spirit-led life.

But there is another desire that is not from the Heavens and it is awakened upon disconnection from God—a sensation called *"sensual desire"* and it has no boundaries, and that is why disconnected humans become larger and larger, become more drunk, more immoral, lazier, more lustful, more self-focused, too talkative, more full of pride, etc., depending upon their vice. Notice this progression… If you close your eyes and ears to God, this causes antiauthority or defiance, which leads to unplugging, which leaves a void that awakens a sensual yearning—a greed or lust. LUCIFER did not warn Adam and Eve of this covetousness. When connected to God, you see that needed boundaries are generous, protective, and perfect for health and relationships. But once disconnected from God, the opposite progression can move at the speed of light. Indeed, before the SATANIC conversation, Adam and Eve had never desired worldly wisdom or power, yet how quickly they desired to "be like God" with omnipotence and power—from grateful to greedy with a move of the eyes... They *saw* that the fruit was desirable... [1] Adam and Eve ignored or turned off the Spirit's prompting and stepped into the sensual.

Since sensual desire is in the head and is generated by the person—not God—there are no shut-off valves. Once man decides

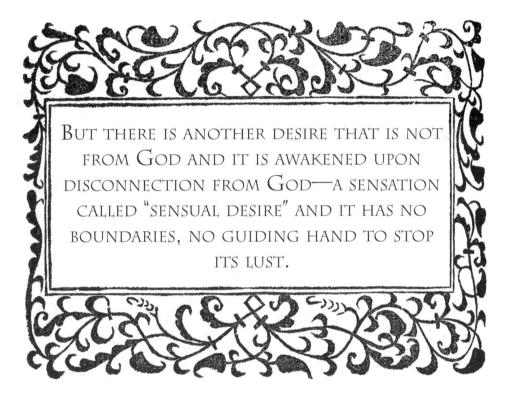

BUT THERE IS ANOTHER DESIRE THAT IS NOT FROM GOD AND IT IS AWAKENED UPON DISCONNECTION FROM GOD—A SENSATION CALLED "SENSUAL DESIRE" AND IT HAS NO BOUNDARIES, NO GUIDING HAND TO STOP ITS LUST.

to disconnect and be his own guide, he had better think twice, for I warn you that man has no built-in feelings to stop—no boundaries—and the sensual grows at a fast rate, just like cancer cells grow faster than normal cells. That is why people will eat or drink until they pass out, blab or entertain pride until they have no friends or wife or have lost their job, smoke until they die of cancer, or lust until they are divorced, bankrupt, and separated from their children.

---

1   *Genesis 3:6*

It is so dangerous to play around with sensual desires, for it is impossible to please the craving. You will never be satisfied and only the grave will stop this LUST–FORCE. As the Apostle Paul says, there is a continual lust for more.[1] People who have no fear need to open their eyes and see that this is a fire that will burn them up. Man is fooling around with something that is way over his head—a good place to wake up and realize... you are not a god and 𝕿𝖍𝖊 𝕮𝖗𝖊𝖆𝖙𝖔𝖗'𝖘 ways are far above the created's ways.

It is time to be on guard for ЅATAN, because he is the one who skillfully introduced "no authority/no boundaries." He is the slick liar who will fill the head with every excuse in the Universe until man drowns in his own sensual desires. ЅATAN has had centuries to create excuses so that they are now immeasurable. All children are taught at a young age the dangers of high places, playing in the street and with fire—but have had no training by the false church leaders to detect the difference between THE SPIRIT and the sensual. This has been the death of the Church. Where are the Teachers? Where are the barking Shepherds?[2] So much pain could have been avoided with proper training. Parents... prioritize your training. Spiritual training is more essential than the ABC's and should be freely talked about.

WHAT IS THIS YOU HAVE DONE?

For Adam and Eve, it all happened so fast and it was so unusual—a first and very new sensation of sensual desire, the original awkward awareness of nakedness and the first time to experience the emotion of fear. What did Adam and Eve do with the realization of rebellion?

---

1   *Ephesians 4:19*
2   *Isaiah 56:10*

They panicked, ran, and hid from God. Later in the evening, they were questioned…"What is this you have done?… Have you eaten from the tree I commanded you not to eat from?" Adam blamed the woman, and the woman projected and said, "The serpent deceived me, and I ate."

How did God know that they had unplugged from Him? How did God know that they had set aside THE SPIRIT and picked up sensual desires? Well, if you know what to look for, it is easy to detect. What is it? All of the sudden, the world centered on them— they were self-focused, hiding from God and looking at their bodies.[1] Toddlers are so focused on the eyes of their parents that they are unaware of themselves and their clothing, or their lack thereof. Take your eyes off God and you become overly self-absorbed. Babies can go from looking at you for everything so that they cry when you walk from the room… to another stage of "Look at me, look at me!" to the point that they never look back to the parent… spoiled. There should be nothing but full respect for authorities while learning to discern if God is guiding you through them. God teaches us to look at Him and all He is, does, and creates. It is an endless banquet for the brain, and since it provides all wisdom for history and all direction and guidance for the future, there is no reason not to focus on The Good Director all day and night! Innocence is defined as wholly focused on God.

Now look at this frightening progression… Lies divert the eyes from "God-focused" to "self-engrossed." This absorption opens the door for SATAN'S lies of victimization, which results in disconnecting and then leads to greed for self. Yes, a frightening progression, but it gets worse… from greed to sensual desires. Sensual desires have no restraint regulator so it is like stepping into the twilight zone—no

---

1   *Genesis 3:6-13*

footing, no direction, no grounding, no boundaries—which moves one into the realm of the unpredictable… gambling with death itself. Worldwide statistics confirm that mankind has entered the twilight zone of no connection and no boundaries—lost in space.

So what was the result of the first sin? The answer is that instead of a healthy, happy, productive relationship with The Creator, man had digressed into bent-over, fear-filled beings, hidden behind a bush… sewing fig leaves.

THE PROTECTION OF AUTHORITY

When God found Adam and Eve, He addressed the authority line. He questioned the man first, and then the woman. How do

you know that Adam's eyes were off of God? You know because the man was with the woman, took direction from the woman, and blamed the woman. Likewise, how do you know the eyes and ears of Eve were off of Adam and God? Eve was listening to the words of SATAN and focused on the fruit and its potential power. If Adam and Eve had been connected and worried about the Connection as they should have been, they would have taken personal responsibility and not blamed the subordinate. People who are connected examine their own responsibility, while people who are disconnected project/blame others for everything—they are never wrong.

Adam and Eve had ushered in the unspeakable—reversing their focus from up to down and therefore annulling or invalidating their authority. It is clear that each upheld a subordinate—Adam was looking to Eve, Eve was looking to LUCIFER, and LUCIFER was looking at himself.[1]

Rejecting the offer of the *life force* through authorities is a foolish choice, but it is, after all, something not mandated—it is your choice... eternal life or eternal death. If you want to end it all, you can—but remember, it has an unfortunate end.

MAN IS NOT A GOD

All those who are not deluded know that they are not a god—and clearly see God as the only Source of electricity. Every time you see pride, know that SATAN is near, for it is LUCIFER who tells you that you are electric. Do not be deceived—flattery is from SATAN. Correction and sober redirection are from good Shepherds. With every decision to ignore one of God's sweet commands, you are unknow-

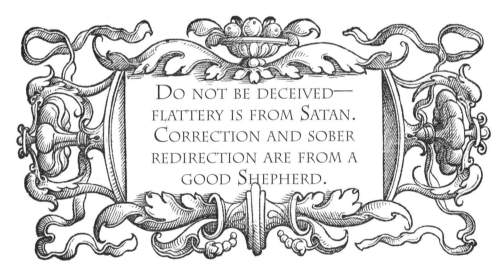

DO NOT BE DECEIVED—
FLATTERY IS FROM SATAN.
CORRECTION AND SOBER
REDIRECTION ARE FROM A
GOOD SHEPHERD.

ingly taking the crown off the only King of All—and crowning yourself as the god. In 586 B.C., the Preacher Ezekiel warned of the end results of this choice... *"This is what the Sovereign Lord says: In*

---

1   *Genesis 3:1-13*

the pride of your heart you say, 'I am a god; I sit on the throne of a god in the heart of the seas.' But you are a man and not a god, though you think you are as wise as a god… but because you think you are wise, as wise as a god… you will die a violent death in the heart of the seas." (Ezekiel 28:2, 6, 8)

Upon listening to lies, SATAN, Adam, and Eve each felt like a god. Eve was spellbound, and with a new false confidence took some of the forbidden fruit and ate it. She also gave some to her husband (who was with her instead of working the Garden), and without hesitation, he ate it. Adam and Eve had been handed food from 𝔊od since their creation—𝔊od gave it to Adam and Adam gave it to Eve. With one small chat, SATAN fed Eve and Eve fed Adam. Upside-down authority—just like that! Up is down and down is up... role reversal, authority reversal, Reality Reversal. Without knowing, the world is looking to SATAN—SATAN is ruling the Earth!

THE RESULT OF THE FIRST SIN ON EARTH

It is unfortunate for the scoreboard that man so quickly wanted to "be like 𝔊od."[1] People grabbing for more reinforces SATAN'S slander on 𝔊od and makes Him look like a stingy provider. Each time you throw off the yoke of authority, SATAN taunts and it just dims the light on the TRUTH of this wonderful, free opportunity while giving a completely false advertisement to the haunted dark side. Danger surrounds man and his family but there are no warnings. The seeker of eternal life cannot be told enough of how hypnotic the power of slander is and how enticing the desire to feel sorry for self is. Would you drink poison if someone handed it to you?—Then why do you listen to people who feel sorry for themselves? People

---

1   *Genesis 3:5*

Outside the prolific Garden there would be more trials and difficulties in man's occupation, so he would be forced into looking more to the Heavens. Because of the curse, the woman would have more of a domestic focus due to the pain of childbearing and the role of the husband.

who complain are slandering God and separating the poor lambs from their food so that most people are starving for *the Connection*. Notice that from Genesis to Revelation, God warns that neither a complainer nor a slanderer can ever enter the Kingdom of God.[1] In fact, any continual sin makes the ridiculous look possible—that the parasite can rule the The Host. Complainers are aiding the dark side and encourage people to take their eyes off of God and encourage the unsuspecting to grab while the grabbing is good. This

---

1   *Numbers 11:1, Numbers 21:4-6, I Corinthians 10:9-11, Jude 1:14-16*

is deadly. Stay away from complainers, slanderers, and the greedy.[1]

Could all of this have been just the downfall of being first—the first man and woman with the first test? Yes—and perhaps that is why God had mercy and gave them a chance to be restored. But we must pay close attention to the steps of restoration if we would like the same consideration. Notice that, number one... Adam and Eve did not stay in the presence of LUCIFER but ran away and hid. Number two... they answered the voice of God when He called and stopped listening to the lies. Both of these decisions saved their lives.[2]

GOD'S RESCUE PLAN

As far as God's decree, the Ancient Scripture states the following:

So the LORD God said to the serpent, "Because you have done this, "Cursed are you above all the livestock and all the wild animals! You will crawl on your belly and you will eat dust all the days of your life. And I will put enmity between you and the woman, and between your offspring and hers; he will crush your head, and you will strike his heel."

To the woman he said, "I will greatly increase your pains in childbearing; with pain you will give birth to children. Your desire will be for your husband, and he will rule over you."

To Adam he said, "Because you listened to your wife and ate from the tree about which I commanded you, 'You must not eat of it,' "Cursed is the ground because of you; through painful toil you

---

1   I Corinthians 5:11
2   Genesis 3:8

will eat of it all the days of your life. It will produce thorns and thistles for you, and you will eat the plants of the field. By the sweat of your brow you will eat your food until you return to the ground, since from it you were taken;

If an enormous dragon breathed fire on you, would you become terrified and run? How much more the Dragon from Hades that breathes lies and offers thoughts to arouse the lustful flames that burn the soul!

for dust you are and to dust you will return." (Genesis 3:14-19)

Only SATAN would see this loving judgment as devastating, for it was the perfect diagnosis and protocol to reconnect Adam and Eve. God repaired the root problem—a lack of focus. It was a focus problem, which created both lack of appropriate appreciation and anti or reversed authority. Because man chose to focus on the woman and the woman focused on LUCIFER'S offer, God chose banishment from the paradise atmosphere. Outside the prolific Garden there would be more trials and difficulties in man's occupation, so he would be forced into looking more to the Heavens.

So what you hear (lies) and what you see... Oh, be careful little ears what you hear; be careful little eyes what you see! Because of the curse, the woman would have more of a domestic focus due to the pain of childbearing and the role of the husband. SATAN was cursed to always crawl on his belly so that everyone was above him, and he would be forced into looking up—and God would put strife between woman and the snake, making it harder to get her attention, for she would disdain him more. Both had to suffer. And what does man do when he suffers?—He cries out to God, thus repairing *the Connection*. It was just like The God of Love and Mercy to show He still cared by redirecting man back to the *life source*. God had not given up on man. When God disciplines a man—He loves the man.[1]

THE GREATEST DAMAGE

On this dark day, two unsuspecting humans took their eyes and ears off of The Source and authority and opened up their ears to SATAN. Once their eyes moved... SATAN could close their eyes to the abundance and open their eyes to the one thing they could not have. They were not victims, nor were they missing anything except a train accident, a plane crash, or a shipwreck—and missing conversing with the GRIM REAPER and missing a funeral service and burial for their souls. But the greatest collateral damage done in this first attack was distorting the word "authority"—changing it to "oppression," thus removing the faith and trust in God providing. The once beautiful word that Angels would have paid good money for... "authority"... had turned into an irritating concept. Yet in reality, earthly authorities were a part of *the Connection*.

Who would have thought that SATAN as the GREAT DRAGON would come to Earth and dissipate and evaporate into a cloud of lies that float around your head—with smoke and mirrors creating such a delusion? If the TRUTH can be penetrated and the hell-bent lie can enter Paradise in the first few hours of the creation of the

---

1   *Hebrews 12:5-11, Proverbs 3:12*

world—how well saturated do you believe that it is after thousands of centuries? Beware… antiauthority unplugs the world.

Do you forget to pray or ignore the Great Battle and forget the role of SATAN? Then you are right where SATAN wants you. Do you think you are exempt from the lies, have never heard a voice, or that the lies are just heard by the mentally ill? Do you believe that the evil forces are not after your soul? Then you are asleep to reality. Wake up! If an enormous dragon breathed fire on you, would you become terrified and run? How much more the DRAGON from Hades that breathes lies and offers thoughts to arouse the lustful flames that burn the soul! The solution is to follow the footsteps of recovery... Adam and Eve ran away from the self-confident buzz that SATAN gave them and fearfully and humbly sought after their Father again.

Therefore, when you are tempted, listen to Heaven's voice and run to fill up on God and His Kingdom, for that will eradicate the emptiness and boredom. The pursuit of purity and eternal peace is fulfilling.

Some people feel trapped in their forbidden behavior. But do not despair, The Creator has great mercy—He still wants this Connection with you. It is called "grace" to reconnect. The prodigal son can step out of the twilight zone, return home, and humbly ask to be under the roof of The Father again.

The TRUTH is, it is a dream opportunity of free but priceless guidance from an invisible Spirit—there for the good of all—something that Adam and Eve almost threw away. It takes my breath away, and the thoughts make my body melt into a position of praise and worship—from standing with arms lifted to the Heavens to prostrate before Him. I crave this authority more than food—seek it like one who will pay any price to find life and peace.

THE RESULT OF SIN

In the end, as a result of this first Cosmic Battle on Earth, you find that SATAN'S bite released enough poison to do damage—but it was not enough to completely sever *the Connection*. God's anti-venom restored the focus, the authority line, and therefore the essential flow of The Spirit. Adam and Eve had desired a whole new world and they got one—but not the one they had been promised by the liar LUCIFER. They did not move up—they were banished from Paradise. Life would include suffering, and it would be harder to access God. Adam and Eve were once directly under and could communicate directly to God, but outside of Paradise they would have to learn to be under worldly authorities and communicate indirectly or through mediators, and it would be centuries before the perfect mediator would come—Jesus Christ.

When God pronounced the curse for the SERPENT, he slithered back into his cave with his drooling demons to prepare an assault on man at another time and another place. LUCIFER would make it his job to know the name and vice of each and every person born. He was many things, but he was not lazy. He was a slave driver, for his demons would work day and night until they could get close to each human—so close that they could use their trusty weapons of lies and flattery once again. The War of Good versus Evil was far from finished! ❧

With one small chat, Satan fed Eve and Eve fed Adam. Upside-down authority—just like that! Up is down and down is up... role reversal, authority reversal, Reality Reversal. Without knowing, the world is looking to Satan—Satan is ruling the Earth!

After God drove man out, He placed on the east side of the Garden of Eden Cherubim and a flaming sword, flashing back and forth, to guard the way to the tree of life.

The Cain Test

CHAPTER 5

After God drove man out, He placed on the east side of the Garden of Eden Cherubim and a flaming sword, flashing back and forth, to guard the way to the tree of life.[1] God had expected more out of man, and He wanted man to be "set apart" for God alone. "Set apart for God" was also referred to as being "holy."

SATAN with his demons stopped at nothing to separate, and would tempt man, using all their powers. Temptation was allowed here on Earth to assess the heart. It was essential to know the weak points to protect the soul. SATAN and his demons made it their number one job to know the name and the weak points of each man, woman, and child. SATAN did this to isolate and then separate man from God— The Source of All Love. And yet God's Angels also knew each

---

1   *Genesis 3:24*

Saint, but instead of learning these facts to flatter and destroy, they learned details to build and strengthen *the Connection*. For LU-CIFER it was temptations; for God it was tests. Just as scar tissue from old wounds leaves the skin stronger, these tests, if man made it through them, would leave them stronger in the end. This first test did exactly that for Adam and Eve. The entire experience with this paradise pet that turned out to be a deadly dragon had been most traumatizing. It was so deeply etched into the brain and the heart, and they would do whatever it took to avoid this phony, fake liar.

NEW RULES WITH REASONS

Now note that God moved man out of the paradise environment so that he would undergo more grieving. The betrayal and the necessary discipline and banishment were heartbreaking to God, but The Source of All Wisdom and Love knew what He had to do to help mankind stay focused and thus connected. New rules with reasons… man was moved from the abundant Garden of Eden, and he was given a harder ground to work. Therefore, man could not be successful without daily intervention from The Father, thus building daily communication. With this new scenario, there was less "free time" inside 24 hours. Man would get to enjoy the Earth but not have so much vacation time—less time to get in trouble. Hard work has a way of facilitating the focus and single-mindedness on The Source.

After the banishment, things would be different in that God would be invisible, and Adam would have to seek and search more for God's face and favor. Adam would not see God walking in the Garden, but the good news was that God did not completely remove His presence. In time, man would readjust to the invisible, and the spiritually connected could almost feel God by his side from time to time. This awe-inspiring appreciation is what man had misplaced in Paradise, and now if Adam could just sense His lead or even catch a glimpse of His smile from the Heavens, it would create a flood of appreciation in the heart, the thing that they had taken for granted at one time. The fall of man had left such an impression that Adam and Eve never wanted to touch pride ever again, be disconnected again,

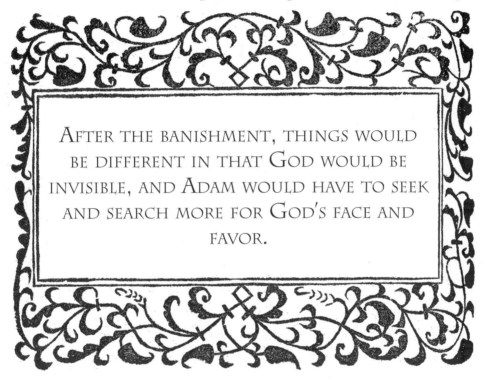

AFTER THE BANISHMENT, THINGS WOULD BE DIFFERENT IN THAT GOD WOULD BE INVISIBLE, AND ADAM WOULD HAVE TO SEEK AND SEARCH MORE FOR GOD'S FACE AND FAVOR.

and certainly never lose favor with The Most High God—no more shorts in the electrical lines that connected them both. God's disappointment was the worst experience in the world.

THE FIRST FAMILY

Later, Adam and Eve had their firstborn son and named him Cain. Eve was reconnected to God, so in humility she said, *"With the help of the LORD I have brought forth a man."*[1] Later she gave birth to his brother Abel. This was the first family, and Cain and Abel grew to manhood. Cain worked the soil like his father—he was a farmer; but Abel herded the flocks.

Now Adam and Eve adored God, and part of what God had taught them to do was to stay appreciative and to give back some of what had been given them. This was an excellent exercise for the heart of every man, woman, and child. The way it worked was that you literally counted your blessings or took inventory of what God had lavished upon you. You then divided it into tenths, and then brought a tenth back to God as an offering. It was really a misnomer to call this an offering or a sacrifice, as if you actually sacrificed something you had given yourself or that you had created. Since it was all a gift in the first place, this was more like payments on borrowed riches. This was never about giving to God, for The Source of All needed nothing. Rather, this was a regular accounting of all that God had given to them and done for each of them, to maintain the essential characteristic of appreciation, which, of course, maintained *the Connection* to the *life force*. So man would literally consider all gifts (as if spreading them out) and then divide them into tenths. One tenth was given at the appreciation service. A holy Saint would love to bring in the tithe because it was evidence of how much you had been blessed. Everything God asked for was only to help man strengthen his connection—a selfless offer!

So in God's genius, the banishment and redirection had

1   *Genesis 4:1-4*

reconnected Adam and Eve, and they now looked for God's lead, His guiding Spirit, morning, noon, and night. It was automatic to stay focused up for everything. But the main thing they looked to Him for was favor, for it was like a meter to read the strength of this all-important Connection. Favor was what they almost lost through antiauthority. Favor was one of the essential blessings of the Connection and made life worth living. Its absence left a great void in the heart of man—leaving a poor soul feeling empty, lonely, and hopeless. Seeking this life-giving water motivated man to get up every day, and it was a good desire that filled the soul. But LUCIFER knew that the unfulfilled void would make man go crazy and create greed for many vices, as well as eventually causing hate, chaos, manslaughter, and suicide.

LUCIFER TARGETS THE CHILDREN

Now, LUCIFER had waited in the background where it concerned Adam and Eve, for their Connection with God was growing stronger every day; and both Adam and especially Eve now disdained not only a seed of pride but also LUCIFER and would run from his presence. The OLD SNAKE had no idea his well-thought-out attack would backfire and wind up making the "man/God" Connection stronger in a roundabout way. This was curious, and LUCIFER could not figure it out, thinking it random. And because he could never connect to TRUTH, he was undeterred and just kept plotting the next victim. But one thing he did know was that he loved children. Children were so much better prey, for they were unaware and also whiny, readily pouting or feeling sorry for themselves. So LUCIFER and his demonic forces hung around Cain and Abel.

Now Cain and Abel had been such a blessing of healing for Adam and Eve. Children got their mind off their huge, huge, shameful mistake in the Garden. Children are such a source of joy to the family that most parents do not want to ever dampen their enthusiasm. Therefore they were not inclined to bring back up past humiliating temptations and lost battles or stories of LUCIFER and his deceitful trap in Paradise. But they did teach their children the joy of authority, and Abel loved to stay focused on 𝕿𝖍𝖊 𝕾𝖔𝖚𝖗𝖈𝖊 𝖔𝖋 𝕬𝖑𝖑, never looking to the right or the left, even though he was the younger brother.

Now, Cain was aware of LUCIFER—yet recently he had grown more and more skeptical of the danger of the OLD SNAKE, for he had never really seen him rebel or be divisive; so he left more and more battle armor at home. This lack of preparation would turn out to be a grave mistake. It all started when Cain had judgmental thoughts, and he really did not think much of it. The twisted thoughts were so random and spaced apart that they were not alarming enough to tell the folks. He used to bring everything to his earthly authority, his dad, and they were very close at one time, but this had changed with physical maturity. Cain wanted some space and independence.

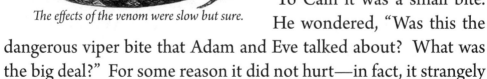

Now, one day while working the garden, the OLD SNAKE who was hiding behind the leaves of the vegetables jumped out, struck and bit Cain's arm with full force. To Cain it was a small bite. He wondered, "Was this the dangerous viper bite that Adam and Eve talked about? What was the big deal?" For some reason it did not hurt—in fact, it strangely

The effects of the venom were slow but sure.

felt good. Cain did not think too much of it, and he had a warm feeling come over him as his eyes opened to the work of his own hands. The crops that were once a gift from 𝕲𝖔𝖉 were now a result of his ingenious farming techniques. Cain felt pride in his work. In fact, he thought for the first time that his work appeared superior to his father's harvests. From this point forward he commenced to put more faith in his own ideas than in the guidance of 𝔱𝔥𝔢 𝔣𝔬𝔯𝔠𝔢, who often gave tips through his earthly authority. Whereas growing up, everybody put all produce in one pile and all used as needed, Cain felt selfish ambition to start his own pile, for he no longer wanted to share his crops. The effects of the venom were slow but sure. Prayer, which was at one time constant, seemed to be more of a rule or religious ritual than an interchange for essential daily direction. Adam and Eve as parents had not picked up on anything other than that Cain seemed to be more to himself, talked less about what 𝕿𝖍𝖊 𝕾𝖔𝖚𝖗𝖈𝖊 was revealing to him, and talked more about his

God made it clear, if YOU change and get it right like Abel, then you can have the favor back, the Connection back, and the smile back on your face. This is Pure Religion.

own business ideas, how to work more efficiently, and how to grow the business. He was not as enthusiastic about the times that they gathered together to talk about how great God was. The voices from the dark side now filled his head with false flattery thoughts of his own gifts and self-importance.

THE UNFAVORED OFFERING

In the course of time, at one of the appreciation gatherings, when the family had counted all that God had given them, Abel joyfully brought the tenth of fat portions from some of the best firstborn of his flock. He could not *wait* to proclaim the miracle of following God's lead with his everyday work, and display and demonstrate the generosity of God—for the bigger the offering, the more glory to God. But a voice from the dark side suggested that Cain hold back, "Save up so you grow the business—after all, you could give more later." So Cain brought a reduced portion

So Cain brought a reduced portion of the fruits of the soil as an offering to the Lord, which did not reflect all that had been given. He misrepresented God and made God look stingy.

of the fruits of the soil as an offering to The Lord, which did not reflect all that had been given. He misrepresented God and made God look stingy. Now the Ancient Scriptures say the following:

"The Lord looked with favor on Abel and his offering, but on Cain and his offering he did not look with favor. So Cain was very angry, and his face was downcast. Then the LORD said to Cain, "Why are you angry? Why is your face downcast? If you do what is right, will you not be accepted? But if you do not do what is right, sin is crouching at your door; it desires to have you, but you must master it." (Genesis 4:4-7)

CAIN'S RESPONSE TO CORRECTION

Instead of The Great I Am cutting Cain off, He gave him the perfect advice… "Sin is crouching at your door; it desires to have you, but YOU must master it."[1] This advice, if heeded, would have saved him from all the grief that was about to occur. But with both radios on—the message was blurred! Cain remained downcast, which means depressed. Notice that the lack of favor from God is the source of depression. The lack of favor from God makes a man depressed. God did not offer Cain antidepressants or pills but rather… TRUTH and redirection to personal responsibility. That was the solution to depression. God made it clear… you change and get it right, and then you can have the favor back, *the Connection* back, and the smile on your face back. This is simple. This is clear. This is PURE RELIGION.

Now at least Cain could still hear what God said, but it was not penetrating. Cain was close enough to God that he could sense the

---

1   *Genesis 4:7*

lack of favor on his behavior. At least Cain was looking for favor, but he was also listening to the ANCIENT SERPENT and wanting his own sensual desires. SATAN'S poison said... "You will be happier if you fulfill your lust for money." If not quickly treated with the anti-venom of TRUTH, this poison will always paralyze its prey—so SATAN bit again. This time it was not an attack on The Creator's authority—Cain had heard that lesson before. It was a new attack... the venom of jealousy, projection, and judgment toward the created, his fellow man. Cain had lost the ability to look inward and be convicted, and this leads to a sure death. He was unable to receive cor-

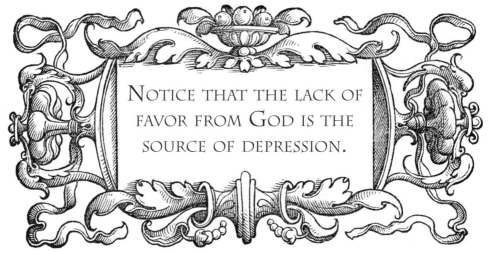

NOTICE THAT THE LACK OF FAVOR FROM GOD IS THE SOURCE OF DEPRESSION.

rection. The heart that is impenetrable just projects outward—but not just projects... I have seen this—it spews; it spits out judgments in a bitter way. He was not just mad because God did not look with favor on his offering, but he was mad because God *did* look with favor on Abel's offering. He was jealous! LUCIFER whispered, "It is Abel's fault. He is making you look bad." LUCIFER used the following concept: Abel made an "A" on the test, and Cain made a "C" or an "F" on the test. If one could just get rid of the "A" student, then God would curve the test and Cain's "C" would be an "A." All the demons turned loyalty into evil as they used twisted thoughts that his downfall was the fault of the sweet-talking, falsely flattering, show-off goody goody!

Saints who were not blinded by the hate could see through Cain's nasty judgmentalness and could see the truth about Abel, that this Holy Saint had set apart his heart, his soul, his mind, and his strength to serve God alone. His offering was an outpouring of an adoring relationship with God. In fact, Abel had grown to have a great *Connection* with God and could not wait to give his offerings, as they were opportunities to be the apple of God's eye. Some would call this concept "faith." On the other hand, Cain was covered over with pain and whispering demons. He had opened the door, so his depression quickly turned to anger. Cain had listened to LUCIFER so much that he was sure that God had misjudged—he had done nothing wrong! He bought the lies... Abel was evil, and his own actions were righteous... Abel was legalistic and therefore a threat to God's religion... Abel was hurting his good reputation. LUCIFER had done it again—good was evil, and evil was appropriate judgments. The god of this world had blinded again![1]

THE FIRST MURDER

So on a very dark day, Cain was eaten up with jealousy, and he said to his loving, unsuspecting brother Abel, *"Let's go out to the field."*[2] It would be the last day on Earth for Abel. It was the last day to see his family and the last day Adam and Eve would enjoy his God-fearing presence, for while they were in the field, Cain attacked his brother Abel and killed him... the first murder.

---

1   II Corinthians 4:4
2   Genesis 4:8

Because of the sin of Cain, Adam and Eve lost both sons in one day. One was dead and buried in the ground, and one was banished from home. Oh, the grief of sin... the broken hearts and the sea of tears it brings. This sent a shock wave through the Heavens!

"Then the LORD said to Cain, "Where is your brother Abel?" "I don't know," he replied. "Am I my brother's keeper?" The LORD said, "What have you done? Listen! Your brother's blood cries out to me from the ground." (Genesis 4:9-10) Well, Cain had killed the physical but not the spiritual. Death could not separate God from his beloved Abel.

WHAT HAVE YOU DONE

With the second sin on Earth, God asks the same question: "What have YOU done?" God did not ask Adam and Eve about their parenting. He did not ask what Abel had done. God did not address SATAN this time, for Cain should have been aware of the schemes of SATAN. No! God asked Cain the standard Judgment Day question for all of mankind... "What have YOU done?" Cain, like Adam and Eve, had enough of the blinding venom in him that he forgot that God was omnipresent. So Cain gave an impertinent answer, showing that he had no remorse for murder and was still in the justifiable, judgmental, projection mode.

The perfect and loving God gave the first pronouncement or verdict on the rebellion that led to the first murder...

"Now you are under a curse and driven from the ground, which opened its mouth to receive your brother's blood from your hand. When you work the ground, it will no longer yield its crops for you. You will be a restless wanderer on the earth." (Genesis 4:11-12)

LUCIFER makes it his job to know everything about a potential prey. The ᴀɴᴄɪᴇɴᴛ sᴇʀᴘᴇɴᴛ, the ᴅʀᴀɢᴏɴ, had been watching and waiting for just the right moment for years; and Adam and Eve and Abel did not see this coming. Cain did not see this coming either.

ʟᴜᴄɪꜰᴇʀ knew the Cain syndrome… There was something about man's work that left weak spots to inject the deadly virus of pride. It seemed too easy to just offer flattery, which initiated sensual desire for more—"selfish ambition," the temptation that required disconnection from 𝕿𝖍𝖊 𝕷𝖔𝖗𝖉 𝖔𝖋 𝕬𝖑𝖑. Greed for praise of man, which belongs to 𝕲𝖔𝖉, and greed to make more money, to gather as many riches and cars and technological gadgets as he wanted. sᴀᴛᴀɴ lied and said that you have to hold back on giving to 𝕲𝖔𝖉, and you have to selfishly store up more for yourself. Men praise others because they want others to praise their works—it is called humanism. Cain liked praise for his work but robbed 𝕲𝖔𝖉 of praise due Him.

Lucifer had perfected projection inside Cain to the point that he could not point a finger at himself. Murder is the result of projection. Cain killed his own brother because Cain felt that Abel purposely made him look bad. Abel simply loved God with all his heart.

Cain had created the wrong kind of competition with Abel. Cain had taken the venom and left the path of faith and went down the road of self-preservation. LUCIFER had perfected projection inside Cain to the point that he could not point a finger at himself. Murder is the result of projection. Cain killed his own brother because Cain felt that Abel purposely made him look bad—poor reasoning! Cain would have been better off to let Abel live and just continually try to imitate Abel's behavior until he got it right—mastered the sin in his heart and restored *the Connection* and favor of 𝕲𝖔𝖉.

PROJECTION / JUDGMENTALNESS

Cain killed Abel because he knew down deep that he was not going to change. He would try to change the system of approval first. In other words, Cain wanted to change the laws and the grace of 𝕿𝖍𝖊 𝕮𝖗𝖊𝖆𝖙𝖔𝖗, and was trying to get the 𝕲𝖗𝖊𝖆𝖙 𝕻𝖗𝖔𝖋𝖊𝖘𝖘𝖔𝖗 to curve the test; so he got rid of the "A" student to help the whole class out. Now with Abel gone, or so Cain thought, 𝕲𝖔𝖉 would have sympathy. But little did he know, 𝕿𝖍𝖊 𝕲𝖔𝖉 𝖔𝖋 𝖂𝖎𝖘𝖉𝖔𝖒 does not curve these tests on Earth. Instead, He told Cain *"...sin is crouching at your door. It desires to have you, but you must master it."*[1] SATAN lies to you and says, "You are just human, and it is impossible to do what 𝕲𝖔𝖉 wants you to do, impossible to obey. Obedience is a work, and 𝕿𝖍𝖊 𝕮𝖗𝖊𝖆𝖙𝖔𝖗 does not want you to work."

SATAN has bitten the religious world so much that this lie paralyzes and permeates almost all religions. How can one believe this lie of SATAN? All 𝕲𝖔𝖉 is offering is for you to take His hand so that He can lovingly walk you through the desert of testing to an oasis of life. He is offering His loving hand for *the Connection*. So you

---

1   *Genesis 4:7*

think you cannot be led by the loving hand of God—do you pull back from the hand of life?... It is all too hard?... Would you rather be led by the black control of the GRIM REAPER?

So you think you cannot be led by the loving hand of God—do you pull back from the hand of life?... It is all too hard?... Would you rather be led by the black control of the Grim Reaper?

It seems impossible to miss this TRUTH. Sin is crouching at the door, but you must master this. Quit trying to get God to change and no longer offer His loving hand to pull you out of the fire. Anger, depression—a downcast feeling—come from wanting it both ways. You want your own decisions, with God's favor and His money to back you and to support your sensual desires. You want it both ways—approval of God while playing god. You can find people who will tell you feeling depressed is an illness and out of your control; but just as quickly as depression comes from sin, joy comes from repentance.

CAIN TRIED TO CHANGE EVERYTHING BUT SELF

Yes, Cain changed many things, but not the right thing. Cain chose to challenge God, to talk back to God, to avoid the questions. Cain chose to get rid of the "A" student and murder; and in the end, what Cain and all the persecutors find out from doing this type of thing is that you cannot accomplish your goal by killing righteous people, for their blood cries out. You cannot kill their reputation, nor their Connection with God. They are still going to, with their righteous lives, condemn what you are doing. The message of the Martyrs became even more powerful upon death, and their testimonies speak louder, even today.

Cain wanted two masters, but take it from me—you cannot have it both ways! The biggest reason that God does not rule on Earth today as Jesus has prayed, is that people divide their devotion between The God and their idols.[1] So then they wind up picking and choosing commands or halfway doing what God wants and then playing king of their own lives. That is you being the master. I want to make it clear—God is not ruling you at all. You are in control, and you cannot be a master and have God as your Master at the same time. Jesus said, *"No one can serve two masters. Either he will hate the one and love the other, or he will be devoted to the one and despise the other. You cannot serve both God and money."* (Matthew 6:24)

You cannot get God's favor by sabotaging your competition. You cannot get rid of the genuine articles, the ones that convict and condemn the world. Centuries after the death of Abel, his righteousness speaks on. The Apostle Paul wrote the following... *"By faith Abel offered God a better sacrifice than Cain did. By faith he was commended as a righteous man, when God spoke well of his offerings. And by faith he still speaks, even though he is dead."*[2] This was the second assault of the great Battle of the Ages—good versus evil.

---

1   *Matthew 6:10*
2   *Hebrews 11:4*

Cain had lost the ability to look inward. He was unable to receive correction. The heart that is not connected to God is impenetrable and just projects the pain to someone else... from anger all the way to murder.

How Do You Change?

How do you resist Lucifer and this temptation to project and then judge? How do you go from being a Cain to being an Abel? If you do what is right, will you not be accepted?[1] Of course you will! But on the other hand, the reverse is true. If you do not do what is right, you will never change! Sin is crouching at your door; it desires to have you, but you must master it.

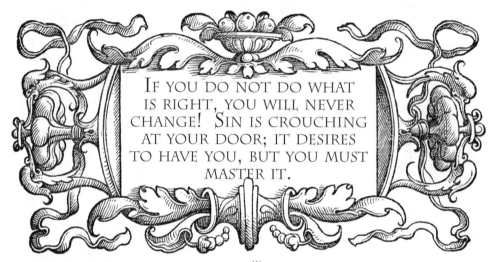

IF YOU DO NOT DO WHAT IS RIGHT, YOU WILL NEVER CHANGE! SIN IS CROUCHING AT YOUR DOOR; IT DESIRES TO HAVE YOU, BUT YOU MUST MASTER IT.

Abel obeyed because he loved God, and Cain struggled with the sacrifice because he loved himself more than God, and therefore did not pass the test.

Many of us have the Cain syndrome so that we give to God what we want to give, not what He asks for. We get angry at God for asking us to sacrifice the thing we love. Moreover, just as Cain did, we get angry at God for not being happy with what we have decided to give Him. If you do not do what is right—the desires and the demons will come near you. They will insert their venom, and they will master you. They will own you and ruin your life on Earth and your *Connection*

---

1   *Genesis 4:7*

with eternity. Doing right is the secret power! If you do what is right, however, you will not judge, and you will master it.

Remember what Jesus said: *"You have heard that it was said to the people long ago, 'Do not murder, and anyone who murders will be subject to judgment.' But I tell you that anyone who is angry with his brother will be subject to judgment."* (Matthew 5:21-22) You see, the reason judgmentalness is so wrong is that it is murder in the heart, which comes from the evil one; and it shows you are disconnected. You must reverse this. You must repent. You must get connected to the love, and that is how you master this. How else do you master it? Again, listen to what God is saying. It is profound! The first four chapters of Genesis give you everything that you need to make it. It is doing what is right! Do you want *the Connection?* Do what is right! Take God's hand and let Him guide you.

REDIRECTION OF CAIN WITH A PURPOSE

Upon the first sin in the Garden and the first redirection, Adam had more suffering with his work—but at least he had a job. But now Cain's redirection would be that he basically could have no successful job anymore—no fruitful employment—nothing prosperous. He would be like the homeless—a vagabond, wandering around—restless. What was God doing? God was redirecting Cain with a purpose. God was removing the source of the pride—the job. Remember, if pride is eradicated, SATAN'S whispers are nothing but wind, and then your eyes will stay on the Heavens where they belong. Cain then could look back on this experience and say, "If only I could have a *Connection* again so that I could work even a humble garden—I would give more than the full tithe of what I have been given!" Losing everything has a way of turning the worst judgmental, jealous person into a humble sojourner who is focused on his own salvation and grateful, positive indebtedness to God— appreciative of the smallest thing. In other words, one would have restored appreciation and restored authority.

Both sins of the first family would be used for the next generations so that mankind could avoid the pride of Cain. As stated over 1,500 years later by our brother John, in I John chapter 3 verse 12: *"Do not be like Cain, who belonged to the evil one and murdered his brother. And why did he murder him? Because his own actions were evil and his brother's were righteous."*

All along, the irony is that God was there to give life to man; the FALLEN ANGEL was there to offer death through various ways. In SATAN'S murderous Garden scheme, he would insidiously get Adam and Eve to unplug so it would look like an accidental suicide. This works, but better yet, through the "Cain Test," get Cain to unplug and then blame the pain—not on God this time—but other men. Therefore, let men kill themselves and murder and hate men and blame God and man. So whether the Garden Test or the Cain Test, the GREAT DRAGON was on a roll. Putting blame on either God or man would always kill. **Do not be fooled,** SATAN **wants to kill each of us.** SATAN would just have to make sure that he got rid of any voice that put the blame back where it should be—on man—for that would save their soul.

LUCIFER saw that patience and timing were continuing to pay off to make man feel victimized so that he would take matters into his own hands. The Angels, who were in disbelief from the whole event, regrouped and tried to get ready for the future onslaughts of SATAN'S army. LUCIFER, however, quickly spread his demons far and wide and repeated the Garden Attack and the Cain Attack all throughout the Earth. ❧

The Angels, who were in disbelief from the whole event, regrouped and tried to get ready for the future onslaughts of Satan's army.

Evil entered the world through pride—a pride that needs no worshipful connection. By Noah's day, the majority were spiritually dead and dying. Who would have ever thought that just the simple concept of projection would be so evil that it could disconnect the world… bury the world.

The Baptism of Sin

CHAPTER 6

Keep in mind, the population greatly multiplied after Cain went out into the world. By the time that Noah walked the face of the Earth, the disconnection was so pronounced and God's pain was so great that poor God regretted that He had made man.[1] LUCIFER had his darting arrows down pat, and hate was so contagious that there was more evil than good. How did LUCIFER get such an upper hand when God had all the power? LUCIFER looked back at his work and realized the tendency for man to congregate in populous cities made his work faster and easier, for man influenced each other faster than demons could lie.

What else caused this massive corruption? Remember, from the beginning of good versus evil—after the rebellion and the challenge

---

1   *Genesis 6:6-7*

of LUCIFER—God created man. God knew that the SERPENT'S threats and challenges were meaningless, for He was the Sole Source of all power—but He allowed this and used this creation of man to prove that humans, who had been given even less power than the Angels, would freely love Him back.

God gave man dominion over the animals, but LUCIFER was given great power to sway the Earth. God wanted an atmosphere to screen and refine man so that He could find men and women in each generation who would seek *the Connection*. These Saints could rise above both sensual desires and Spiritual Warfare—requirements necessary to live forever. These tests were difficult, to say the least.

THE DOOR OF PAIN

The CRAFTY SNAKE knew the demonic policy of waiting like a spider behind the door until the day of pain. Pain and depression sounded the alarm for all the crouching demons to wake up to make a move. All of LUCIFER'S forces would then take their positions to shoot darting arrows of lies into the mind. Pain is the door. Pain is the open wound of victimization where the venom is easy to inject. That is why Saints need to be there when fellow Saints are in pain. If the pain is not given the TRUTH, the lies cause self-inflicted depression all the way to suicide or projected anger and hate all the way to murder. LUCIFER likes both—the pattern of the pit: from depression to anger, from anger to depression. LEGION and lies crouch behind this door to the heart of man, and if you do not shut the door to the lies and say the TRUTH then sin will master you. What is the TRUTH? "You have everything if you have God." What is the TRUTH? "God is everything." The lies of victimization kill the spirit and turn to murder the Righteous. These tests on Earth are not kindergarten tests. This training ground is a tight sieve to separate good from evil. Much like the Marines, the special Spiritual Elect Army needs to go through much preparation so that they are highly prepared for any spiritual circumstance.

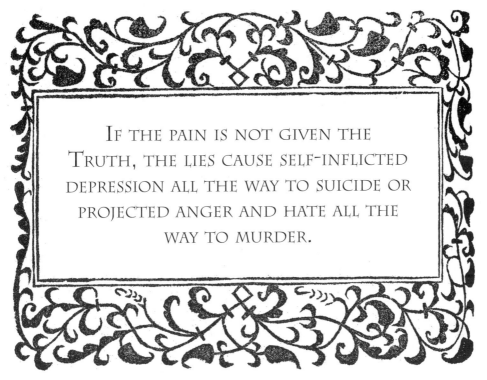

IF THE PAIN IS NOT GIVEN THE TRUTH, THE LIES CAUSE SELF-INFLICTED DEPRESSION ALL THE WAY TO SUICIDE OR PROJECTED ANGER AND HATE ALL THE WAY TO MURDER.

LUCIFER'S challenge provided the perfect sieve for this level of training of the mind and heart of man. Remember the results of unplugging—LUCIFER was both blind and deaf. It is hard to predict what drove this diabolical menace onward. Perhaps he thought that there would be some kind of hope for a reversal of his judgment if he could prove how easy it was to unplug man from God. Who knows all of his twisted motives, other than the obvious hatred and revenge to destroy what God had made—to murder, because he knew that his time was short. You know... you have heard on the news about men who machine-gun down as many innocent bystanders as they can before they save the last bullet for themselves. These men are angry because they are in pain and their lives are a wreck and their time is short, so they try to hurt others. No one in their right mind would have ever challenged God in the first place, so there was no way to reason with or understand The BEAST. Nevertheless, instead of putting this supernatural serial murderer behind bars, God allowed him to continue to stalk mankind.

Remember… the basic device of the sieve was the lie, keeping GENERAL LUCIFER with his warriors so clandestine that mankind would debate and question if demons existed at all, while mocking the concept of the Cosmic Battle. Even the most religious had questioned the supernatural as just a figment of the imagination. This DELUSION grew with each generation, as each generation increasingly underestimated the Warfare and the persuasion of the lies. Oh… but the reality was that TRUTH extends life, yet lies murder mankind. The lie could kill—just like that! How could man not research what kept him alive or what caused his demise?

Again, if man could just study the Garden Lies and how 43 words turned arms that were loaded with blessings into needy arms grabbing for more. These words assured them that nothing would happen to them—they would not surely die. These lies blamed God for their "necessary," "needed" actions. In the Desert of Testing, LUCIFER offered Jesus the following… "You can have the world and worldly power if you bow down and worship me." But Jesus refused it all.[1] For the Cain Lies, the ANCIENT SERPENT had disobedient Cain never look inward—not even for one second—and had him project instead. He believed the source of his pain was due to Abel. Cain believed the lie that another man could actually cause your pain. But that is not true. Projection diverts the life force from

---

1   Matthew 4:8-10

In the Desert of Testing, Lucifer offered Jesus the following… "You can have the world and worldly power if you bow down and worship me." But Jesus refused it all.

you and so ends your spiritual life and then creates hate for others. Lucifer framed God and now he successfully framed a righteous man. The REAL PERPETRATOR could slither away from the hot seat and put God and other men on trial, leaving a world of judgmentalness and hate and murder in the heart of mankind.

SPIRITUAL AND PHYSICAL DEATH

It is essential to understand the following so that all history of mankind can be interpreted correctly: a human has been given two sources of life and two types of death—physical and spiritual. The physical and the spiritual are separate but affect one another. As far as the two lives… there is your physical life, and then there is your spiritual life. Jesus would say that you need to be born again[1]— that is your second or spiritual life.

There is a physical death and a spiritual death. As far as the physical, man is mortal and his days are numbered—determined by God alone.[2] The subject of physical death is blocked or circumvented in the minds of most people. This must be faced because the acceptance or rejection of this TRUTH affects all future decisions and all choices of behavior—it is monumental.

Your spiritual health affects your physical health. There is a direct correlation. The healthier *the Connection*, the healthier the body, as a rule—for obedience to God's rules is there to give you the maximum health (unless God has assigned certain ailments for various reasons). You could be experiencing natural aging physically, but if you are connected to God, your spirit will stay alive, and even physical death cannot kill it.

---

1 John 3:3
2 Job 14:5

However, if you are spiritually dead—disconnected from The Vine—then your physical life will die prematurely. Spiritual death kills both spiritual and physical so that the person is a walking zombie—the walking dead. The smile is a mask that is taken off when away from the public. Underneath is the depression, anger, and hate, unless that person is in the middle of sensual indulgence. Spiritual health is far more important because it helps with the present age and the age to come—it is eternal. Spirit-filled people refer to death as "sleep" and know it is simply a pause—a comma in their existence. They know that they will wake up to more life.

Each disconnected human is inflicting death upon himself and is cutting short his own days. Every sensual indulgence or vice kills the spiritual and the physical—obesity cuts all life short and is the single most related factor to early death because it causes cancer, heart disease, and diabetes. Excess tobacco and alcohol can kill the physical and spiritual. Sexual sins can cause horrific pain and disease and death. Spiritual death causes so much physical and mental pain.

THE SPIRITUAL DEATH IN NOAH'S DAY

During the time of Noah, the original lies had brought complete rebellion to the Connection to The Creator—unplugging most from the life support. In addition, many men were now killing each other. The polytheistic nations were full of zombies, and the cities were essentially graveyards or mortuaries for the spiritually dead. Evil is so contagious, so this evil had rapidly taken over and its poison was doing what LUCIFER had hoped—causing the premature spiritual death and therefore physical death of many. With so much sin, God's pain was great. So after the first two victories of

LUCIFER, the population increased and scattered, and The DRAGON sent LEGION out into the world to repeat the lustful Garden Test and then the projection Cain Test. Worldwide disconnections left a global void, which drove mankind to fill up with sensual desires. The world began swimming with sin. When God saw Noah, a man with his family who would obey all the commands—a Remnant of

Noah was a righteous man, blameless among the people of his time, and he walked with God.

Righteousness—He decided to spare man from complete self-destruction. Once again, God intervened to save a Remnant of mankind by washing away those who had already chosen death and an early death sentence through the greatest storm on Earth.

THE STORY OF THE GREAT FLOOD

From the Holy writings of ancient Prophets in Genesis 6...

"The LORD saw how great man's wickedness on the earth had become, and that every inclination of the thoughts of his heart was only evil all the time. The LORD was grieved that he had made man on the earth, and his heart was filled with pain. So the LORD said, 'I will wipe mankind, whom I have created, from the face of the earth—men and animals, and creatures that move along the ground, and birds of the air—for I am grieved that I have made them.' But Noah found favor in the eyes of the LORD."

"This is the account of Noah. Noah was a righteous man, blameless among the people of his time, and he walked with God. Noah had three sons: Shem, Ham and Japheth. Now the earth was corrupt in God's sight and was full of violence. God saw how corrupt the earth had become, for all the people on earth had corrupted their ways. So God said to Noah, 'I am going to put an end to all people, for the earth is filled with violence because of them. I am surely going to destroy both them and the earth. So make yourself an ark of cypress wood; make rooms in it and coat it with pitch inside and out.'

"'This is how you are to build it: The ark is to be 450 feet long, 75 feet wide and 45 feet high. Make a roof for it and finish the ark to within 18 inches of the top. Put a door in the side of the ark and make lower, middle and upper decks. I am going to bring floodwaters on the earth to destroy all life under the heavens, every creature that has the breath of life in it. Everything on earth will perish. But I will establish my covenant with you, and you will enter the ark—you and your sons and your wife and your sons' wives with you. You are to bring into the ark two of all living creatures, male and female, to keep them alive with you. Two of every kind of bird, of every kind of animal and of every kind of creature

that moves along the ground will come to you to be kept alive. You are to take every kind of food that is to be eaten and store it away as food for you and for them.'

"Noah did everything just as God commanded him. The LORD then said to Noah, 'Go into the ark, you and your whole family, because I

Now the earth was corrupt in God's sight and was full of violence. God saw how corrupt the earth had become, for all the people on earth had corrupted their ways. So God said to Noah, 'I am going to put an end to all people, for the earth is filled with violence because of them. I am surely going to destroy both them and the earth. So make yourself an ark of cypress wood; make rooms in it and coat it with pitch inside and out.' (Genesis 6:11-14)

have found you righteous in this generation. Take with you seven of every kind of clean animal, a male and its mate, and two of every kind of un-clean animal, a male and its mate, and also seven of every kind of bird, male and female, to keep their various kinds alive throughout the earth. Seven days from now I will send rain on the earth for forty days and forty *nights, and I will wipe from the face of the earth every living creature I have made.' And Noah did all that the LORD commanded him."*[1] *"Then the LORD shut him in."*[2]

"And after the seven days the floodwaters came on the earth. In the six hundredth year of Noah's life, on the seventeenth day of the second month—on that day all the springs of the great deep burst forth, and the floodgates of the heavens were opened. And rain fell on the earth forty days and forty nights."[3]

"... as the waters increased they lifted the ark high above the earth. The waters rose and increased greatly on the earth, and the ark floated on the surface of the water. They rose greatly on the earth, and all the high mountains under the entire heavens were covered. The waters rose and covered the mountains to a depth of more than twenty feet. Every living thing that moved on the earth perished—birds, livestock, wild animals, all the creatures that swarm over the earth, and all mankind. Everything on dry land that had the breath of life in its nostrils died. Every living thing on the face of the earth was wiped out; men and animals and the creatures that move along the ground and the birds of the air were wiped from the earth. Only Noah was left, and those with him in the ark.

"The waters flooded the earth for a hundred and fifty days. But God remembered Noah and all the wild animals and the livestock that were with him in the ark, and he sent a wind over the earth, and the waters receded. Now the springs of the deep and the floodgates of the heavens had been closed, and the rain had stopped falling from the sky. The water receded steadily from the earth. At the end of the hundred and fifty days the water had gone down, and on the seventeenth day of the seventh month the ark came to rest on the mountains of Ararat. The waters continued to

---

1   *Genesis 6:5-7:5*
2   *Genesis 7:16*
3   *Genesis 7:10-12*

recede until the tenth month, and on the first day of the tenth month the tops of the mountains became visible.

"After forty days Noah opened the window he had made in the ark and sent out a raven, and it kept flying back and forth until the water had dried up from the earth. Then he sent out a dove to see if the water had receded from the surface of the ground. But the dove could find no

place to set its feet because there was water over all the surface of the earth; so it returned to Noah in the ark. He reached out his hand and took the dove and brought it back to himself in the ark. He waited seven more days and again sent out the dove from the ark. When the dove returned to him in the evening, there in its beak was a freshly plucked olive leaf! Then Noah knew that the water had receded from the

earth. He waited seven more days and sent the dove out again, but this time it did not return to him.

"By the first day of the first month of Noah's six hundred and first year, the water had dried up from the earth. Noah then removed the covering from the ark and saw that the surface of the ground was dry. By the twenty-seventh day of the second month the earth was completely dry. Then God said to Noah, 'Come out of the ark, you and your wife and your sons and their wives. Bring out every kind of living creature that is with you—the birds, the animals, and all the creatures that move along the ground—so they can multiply on the earth and be fruitful and increase in number upon it.' So Noah came out, together with his sons and his wife and his sons' wives."[1]

"Then Noah built an altar to the LORD and, taking some of all the clean animals and clean birds, he sacrificed burnt offerings on it.

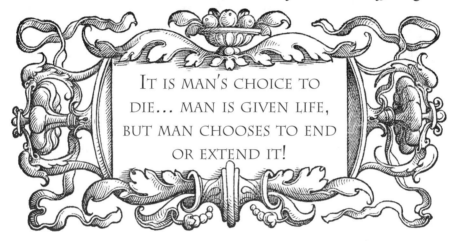

IT IS MAN'S CHOICE TO DIE… MAN IS GIVEN LIFE, BUT MAN CHOOSES TO END OR EXTEND IT!

The LORD smelled the pleasing aroma and said in his heart: 'Never again will I curse the ground because of man, even though every inclination of his heart is evil from childhood. And never again will I destroy all living creatures, as I have done. As long as the earth endures, seedtime and harvest, cold and heat, summer and winter, day and night will never cease.'"[2]

So God sent the greatest storm on Earth known to mankind with warnings, and no one repented. Noah released a dove after the great flood in order to find land. The dove came back carrying an olive branch in its beak, telling Noah the great flood had receded and that there was land once again for man to walk on.

---

1   Genesis 7:17-8:18
2   Genesis 8:20-22

THE MEANING OF THE RAINBOW

After the water receded, God sent the rainbow as a sign of His love for man, that He would not eradicate the walking dead this way again—drowning all the animals at the same time. So He baptized the Earth and buried the spiritually dead and spared those spiritually alive. However, the rainbow was used by LUCIFER to assure all men that The Creator would never destroy man again, adding to the POWERFUL DELUSION. In fact, the rainbow is used by certain sects of sinful people to assure each other that nothing will ever happen to them.

LUCIFER blamed God for what happened, when the TRUTH was that all blame was on man. It cannot be said enough in this world where the lie reigns... that God wants all mortal men to live out their lives and He wants their spirits to live forever! But when man unplugs himself from the life support, he has chosen a sure death. The human race needs to get this straight or they will face a disaster of this proportion again. It is man's choice to die... man is given life, but man chooses to end or extend it! The Selfless Life Source just buried those who had chosen death with the flood and then baptized the Earth of the disconnected to extend the life of the connected.

FROM THE FRUIT OF MANKIND

SATAN and his forces will condemn God and threaten... "How dare The Creator shorten the existence"—no matter how depraved and twisted they are. But The Creator did not create man just so that he could kill himself and then kill others. God made man to live eternally with Him.

LUCIFER was so clever that he was able to keep all blame on God and none on man—no fingers pointed at the humans who were bringing an untimely death to themselves through their own devices… men who had chosen to shorten life through sensual gluttony, alcoholism, sexual lust, pride—anything that disconnected them from their wonderful and holy and blessed Heavenly Father.

The skilled ANCIENT LIAR would take another crowd that never blamed God and say, "A loving God would never do such a thing to man." How do they explain, then, all that has happened? Many claim that the flood is a myth. Another segment of the population ignore commenting on the destruction of civilization through divine retribution and rather recount the story from a child's perspective, with happy rainbows and doves. The majority believe God never sends storms and attribute all natural disasters to "Mother Nature." Yet the Scriptures are clear that He is in control of the winds and the waves.[1] All explanations are so twisted that it makes you question either the existence *or* the vast love of God. Either lie successfully distracts man from the TRUTH of personal responsibility, and that is the most dangerous threat to the existence of man. If Cain can kill Abel, what is to stop man from killing himself or wiping out mankind again with the lies of SATAN?

The TRUTH is our only hope! The TRUTH is that this falsely accused God gives every opportunity for His creation to live forever and to link to His life-giving Source, which extends the physical—a sort of fountain of youth—and gives eternity to the spirit. Never forget, it is God who begs and pleads with man through Scriptures and Prophets to "repent and live!"[2] Like a mother kangaroo with her babies in her pouch or a mother nursing her baby with life-giv-

---

1   Isaiah 54:16, Isaiah 24:18-20
2   Ezekiel 18:30-32, Luke 13:3

ing milk—God is willing to give life to those who want it, with a love deeper than any parent has ever felt.

The Truth is the deliverer of our souls! Notice that when you finally see the Truth, you no longer feel sorry for yourself, but rather your sorrow is in the right place—it is for God. Just imagine a mother giving birth to many children but one by one they commit suicide or kill each other off. It is exceedingly heartbreaking for God. The road to life is narrow.[1] Death has been the choice for most men, for they have been unaware and therefore have underestimated the power of SATAN. The Truth about the rainbow is that God said he would never bury the spiritually dead in a flood—but man is responsible for the destruction of civilization. If man chooses to shorten his own life (take the gift and destroy it), how much more is it The Creator's right to facilitate this choice—especially before man spreads his death choice to others! So this explains how the Earth became the most unnecessary sea of death by the time of Noah. They had all chosen to drown in a sea of lust and hate before the water ever touched the ground. LUCIFER felt very satisfied at being the undisclosed perpetrator behind the manslaughter, but even more pleased with the perfect frame job or setup against The Passionate, Life-giving Source. God appeared like this indiscriminate wrongdoer. LUCIFER planted the most blasphemous and sacrilegious lie: that God was indiscriminately caustic and needed to repent! May this lie evaporate and this Truth permeate the planet and change the world.

Inconceivable Projection

Now you see that it is unthinkable to blame God, and therefore we must never project onto God! Man threw off the life source like

---

1   Matthew 7:13-14

By Noah's day, the majority were spiritually dead and dying. Now God would start over with Noah and his family—a Remnant who understood that the secret of this life force was due to a connection with The Creator.

a patient tearing off the life support or IV bags. God did not take life. It was God and God alone—The Great Physician—who offered life and life support again to Adam and then Eve and then Cain and others. Man sinned first or rejected life. Now we see clearly… it was the ANCIENT SERPENT who tried to exterminate the first man and kill the first children on Earth—unplug young people without knowing that they are unplugged. SATAN and man caused the flood, for they did not know their Creator, nor the created's purpose.

To this day, this POWERFUL DELUSION has been embellished and repeated and it permeates the foundational religious direction of mankind. SATAN, now through false teachers, says that the God of the Old Testament is different than the God of the New Testament. It is blasphemy—that God needed to repent. It is so irreverent to think the unthinkable. How profane to insinuate that God needed to change because of His wrath on men who were destroying His creation, His Earth, His plans, His purpose, His relationships, His dreams, His love, and breaking His Heart! How about God's perspective. After 4,000 years of lies, it is time to feed the world THE TRUTH. God's wrath is from the whole unnecessary waste of life. To the contrary—*man* has got to repent, *man* has got to change, *man* is to blame and he needs to stop destroying what God has made. What God has put together, let no man put asunder!

THE SIN OF DESTROYING WHAT GOD HAS CREATED

Mankind has enough morals to know that it is wrong to tear down someone else's sandcastle. Not one of the millions that will visit the beach this year would put up with such an offense—but so few have enough sense to know how much more not to destroy the body that God has made. How depraved we have become. In I Corinthians 3:16 Paul says, *"Don't you know that you yourselves are God's temple and that God's Spirit lives in you? If anyone destroys God's temple, God will destroy him; for God's temple is sacred, and you are that temple."* You are sacred so you must connect to The Sovereign to care for the sacred. ❧

The Tree of the Knowledge of Good & Evil

The Conclusion

In conclusion to *History of the ONE TRUE GOD Volume I: The Origin of Good and Evil,* God had started off in the Heavens with a one-world religion, all of creation worshipping The One True God—the religion that brings life—the worship that brings eternal life… however, on Earth the POWERFUL DELUSION had altered it into a one-world worship of SATAN and self… the death of Sovereignty—the kiss of death. Evil entered the world through pride—a pride that needs no worshipful connection. By Noah's day, the majority were spiritually dead and dying. Now God would start over with

Noah and his family—a Remnant who understood that the secret of this *life force* was due to the perpetual, reciprocal love and provisions that The Creator gave the Created, and in return, the uninterrupted, complete link of love the Created gave back due to appreciation. How do you know Noah was attached to The Guiding Hand? He did everything God commanded. It is the sign.

Who would have ever thought that just the simple concept of projection would be so evil that it could disconnect the world… bury the world. God is desperately working around the clock to ensure the life of man, but man has been blinded by the poison of The Viper and believed that God did not care and was holding back on man.

Another storm is brewing on this Earth again because of the permeation of Lucifer's lies causing the increase in the choice of sin. It is a wonder that the Earth still spins on its axis, for the globe is filled with lies; lies paralyze change. The church has long lost the ability to detect the difference between The Spirit and the sensual—the *life force* versus the Lust-force. And has mankind ever known that the tree of the knowledge of good and evil was not put there to give man knowledge but to give God knowledge of man's heart? The victory or the defeat of temptation shows man's true colors—the motives of his heart.

The choice of the Lust force guides the majority so Satan is ruling the Earth—but the good news is God rules the Universe! The One and Only God has the secret formula that gives the victory over death. This *life force* is self-perpetuating light, life, and beauty—in other words, the secret to eternity. It is one thing to create life, but another to keep it going.

Not only did this Omnipotent Source hold the secret to His own youth, but out of His generosity, He created Angels and then men and extended this invaluable *life force* so that they could have His Divine Spirit, energy, vitality, enthusiasm, and exuberance to live forever in peace and love. God's intent has always been to provide life with a joyous setting that is way beyond description and imagination. But the world has bought into the lies and cannot see that SATAN has been the perpetrator of wars, chaos, depression, poverty,

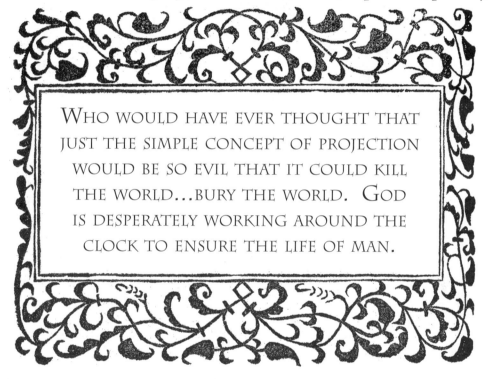

WHO WOULD HAVE EVER THOUGHT THAT JUST THE SIMPLE CONCEPT OF PROJECTION WOULD BE SO EVIL THAT IT COULD KILL THE WORLD...BURY THE WORLD. GOD IS DESPERATELY WORKING AROUND THE CLOCK TO ENSURE THE LIFE OF MAN.

and death. The lie is so strong that they do not even believe that SATAN exists, much less that there is a Cosmic Challenge. But after all, is that not the foundation of THE GREAT DELUSION ... to make the world believe that God is not at war with SATAN ... that there are no demonic rulers, authorities, or powers of the dark world, nor spiritual forces of evil in the Heavenly realms?

But the storms are not to annihilate man but rather to baptize the sin to ensure life for the next generation. It is to provide an environment so that once again a Remnant of those who cling to their Lord God Almighty can thrive. Sin is buried only if needed to continue the species of mankind whom God adores.

LUCIFER was satisfied with the damage inflicted upon God by the great flood, for with a cloud of suspicion on God or Righteous men, no one would ever listen to the TRUTH. But it is the TRUTH that sets you free. It is THE TRUTH that is the answer. The world is in need of a voice of TRUTH to set it free from the clutches of The GREAT DRAGON, from the Reality Reversal, which is the death to Sovereignty. If man would just take these six chapters to heart and mind and see that eternal life is their choice—it is their opportunity—it would save the world by restoring man's responsibility, and perhaps we all would live long enough to go beyond the sin that has brought about the death of Sovereignty to witness...

the days that Sovereignty rises again!

THE END OF VOLUME ONE

Prayer

O Great and Omnipotent God, the One True God, the Lord God Almighty, how amazing beyond amazing you are. You are The Great I Am. You are everything—the Source of all. We are so appreciative that your ways are above man's and that you are all wisdom and all love. Thank you for offering the Connection—it is a gift of living water that we cannot comprehend. We can never thank or repay you enough; we owe you everything. To reject this gift—to reject the life force and the life source—all of life—your Spirit to man, Father, is incomprehensible. We come today humbly before your throne through Jesus Christ, asking, O God, that you forgive us and allow us to connect, reconnect, never again to disconnect from you again. May each man, woman, and child reach out, seek, and knock on the door until the door opens. Father, help us to know that LEGION and lies are crouching at our door. Lead us not into temptation, but deliver us from this EVIL ONE. We pray that we will master the temptations and evil desires. For yours is the Kingdom, yours is the power, yours is the glory—for ever and ever. Always requested through the powerful name of Jesus Christ, your only Son, Amen.

Instead of putting this supernatural serial murderer behind bars, God allowed him to continue to stalk mankind. Remember, Satan never quits; evil never sleeps. Lucifer makes it his job to know the name and vice of each and every person born. His demons work day and night until they get close to each human—so close that they can use their trusty weapon of flattery once again. Spiritual Warfare is real and we must all pray without ceasing for guidance for ourselves and for the spiritual Connections of all Saints around the world.

Appendix

NOTE ABOUT WRITING STYLE

You may notice a difference in the capitalization of certain terms. It has been decided to honor (via capitalization of the first letter) all terms that are referencing God, the Kingdom, His Holy Servants, and The Great Battle. Likewise, you will see a trend toward de-emphasizing (via using lowercase of the first letter) religions not founded by God. Notice "SATAN" and all his diabolical titles will be recognized by an eerie font. I have noticed in modern writings that references to "pharisees," are capitalized, but there is no capitalization of God's Priests or Holy Priesthood!? There are no capitalizations in the Hebrew language. It is an absolute crime that all references to common denominations have ensured capitalization of their organization but there is no capitalization when referencing God's "Church" or The Kingdom of God. Bear with me as I am trying to right this wrong in this prayerful work. These changes are intentional. May other literature follow suit.

NOTE ABOUT BIBLE VERSIONS

As you dig for this wisdom, we encourage you to keep *The Bible* handy to reference all Scripture given. We strongly encourage the use of the New International Version (NIV 1984). The world's top theologians, linguists, and scholars of Hebrew, Aramaic, and Greek spent many thousands of hours researching and discussing the meaning of the original manuscripts and texts, producing perhaps the most thorough and reviewed translation of God's Holy Word to date. Speaking of THE GREAT DELUSION, the revised version of the NIV has changes that flatter versus convict. We do not recommend the Today's New International Version (TNIV) or the 2011 version of the NIV.

NOTE ABOUT ARTWORK

Artists include Gustave Doré, Julius Schnorr von Carolsfeld, Cornelis Floris, Christoph Weigel, Jan Goeree, Casper Luiken, and Erin Shamblin. Some of these images were altered digitally for various purposes and modesty. Digitel editing done by Ryan McCauley and directed by Gwen Shamblin and Erin Shamblin—the graphic arts team.

ABOUT THE AUTHOR

Gwen Shamblin was born and raised in Memphis, Tennessee, with a strong faith and foundational values. She grew up with a medical background, making rounds with her belated father, Walter Henley, M.D., who was a General Surgeon. She received her undergraduate degree in Dietetics and Masters Degree in Nutrition with an emphasis in Biochemistry from the University of Tennessee in Knoxville. Mrs. Shamblin was an Instructor of Foods and Nutrition at the University of Memphis for five years, and she worked with the city's Health Department for an additional

five years, helping specifically in the areas of overweight, obesity, pregnancy, and child health.

A very spiritual person with a strong faith in God, Mrs. Shamblin felt led to found The Weigh Down Workshop in 1986 in order to teach these principles to those who were desperately seeking to lose weight permanently. Initially offered through audiotapes and small classes taught by Mrs. Shamblin in a retail setting, this teaching began yielding unprecedented results. Participants were not only losing their weight while eating regular foods, but they were using the same Bible-based principles to turn away from other addictions such as smoking or alcohol abuse.

By 1992, the program was packaged for seminar use, churches began to sign up, and the media began to pay attention. The growth was explosive. By the late 1990s, Weigh Down was internationally known in most Protestant, Catholic, and Evangelical

churches around the world. Gwen Shamblin and The Weigh Down Workshop were featured on such shows as *20/20*, *Larry King Live*, and *The View*, as well as in such magazines as *Good Housekeeping* and *Woman's Day*. In 1997, *The Weigh Down Diet* was published by Doubleday, Inc. The book quickly sold over one million copies as people discovered the secrets to losing weight quickly and permanently while finding a new relationship with God.

Feeling led to go even further in helping others

to live fully for God, in 1999, Gwen Shamblin, along with other individuals who shared her passion for God, founded the Remnant Fellowship Church. Twice-weekly Church services are webcast live from the original Remnant Fellowship Church located outside Nashville, Tennessee.

The dream of helping people turn away from the love of food and toward a love of God has turned into

a ministry. Through Remnant Fellowship and Weigh Down Ministries, hundreds of people are helped daily as they break away from the pain of obesity and other addictive behaviors. Gwen is continually producing new materials for both the Church and the Weigh Down Ministries, yet she takes no salary for her efforts. Funds that are received through the sale of Weigh Down products

and seminar fees or through donations to the Church are used to support each respectively in order to help hurting people of every nationality discover the love of God that can set them free.

Gwen Shamblin has been married to David Shamblin for well over 30 years. They have two grown children who have children of their own. Their son, Michael, is married to Erin (who is affectionately called Elle), and they have three

daughters... Gabriele, Garland, and Gates. Gwen and David's daughter, Elizabeth, is married to Brandon Hannah, and they have four children... Gracie, Gweneth, Gloria, and Henley. The children and their spouses have always been supportive and work alongside her in the church and their contributions are invaluable.

ADDITIONAL RESOURCES
All available at www.WeighDown.com

Weigh Down Ministries is the non-profit publishing house for and is sponsored by Remnant Fellowship Churches. It has been producing resources for over 30 years which have proven to help participants overcome overeating, alcoholism, gambling, drugs, sexual sins, greed for money, and other strongholds, fully supporting all people seeking to glorify God and promote His Kingdom. If you need help or know someone who needs help, please refer to this list of resources.

BOOKS

∽ HISTORY OF THE *ONE TRUE GOD* COMPLETE SET

This book is Volume One of *History of the ONE TRUE GOD* Series. Please check our website for additional volumes.

∽ WEIGH DOWN DIET

Practical advice to help you on the path from physical hunger to spiritual fulfillment.

∽ RISE ABOVE

Look inward into your own heart and learn to transfer your devotion to the food over to a wholehearted devotion to God Almighty. You truly fall in love with what you focus on, so prepare to change your mindset, which then will change your heart.

∽ THE LEGEND TO THE TREASURE

This book will change the way you evaluate your weight, finances, marriage, and all relationships. Let your eyes be opened to The Treasure and be permanently set free. This book is also used in a 16-week advanced study.

SEMINARS

∽ WEIGH DOWN BASICS

A six-week home study filled with Weigh Down's groundbreaking approach to weight loss. Learn how to replace the greed for food with a passion for God.

∽ EXODUS OUT OF EGYPT: THE CHANGE SERIES

Eight-week seminar. Practical tips, hints, and advice on weight loss and dealing with "problem" foods or tempting situations during the day.

∽ Exodus From Strongholds

Twelve-week seminar. Break free from any stronghold (over-drinking, nagging, anger, drugs, praise of man, etc.) in your life—permanently.

∽ The Last Exodus

Eight-week seminar for ages eight and up. Basic steps to help your children find a relationship with God so that they can grow up with the tools they need to fight any temptation they face, including weight loss. You will want to get your entire family involved in this seminar.

∽ Breakthrough

Eight-week advanced weight loss seminar for those who have plateaued in their weight. This seminar will emphasize personal accountability and responsibility and will help you go all the way.

∽ The Legend to The Treasure

An advanced study—based on nautical symbolism that helps the participant steer his ship in the right direction toward a deeper relationship with God.

∽ Weigh Down Advanced

Ten-week seminar. Discover the root of any remaining pull toward your strongholds and take your relationship with God to the next level.

∽ Feeding Children Physically & Spiritually

Children, parents, and parents-to-be all will benefit from this information. Parents can spare their children a lifetime of overeating, restrictive dieting, and following man-made rules which often lead to anorexia and bulimia as well as overweight.

∽ Zion Kids Series

A collection of videos that will transform the whole household, for it is full of God's music and knowledge of God and worship to Him. Gwen used these principles based upon the Bible's mere Christianity message in raising her own children, Michael and Elizabeth.

WEBSITES & FREE RESOURCES

∽ TRUTHSTREAM

A monthly online subscriber program where you have access to hundreds of life-changing audios and videos from Weigh Down and Remnant Fellowship Church services. Our greatest guidance/training and encouragement tool to date! http://store.weighdown.com/TruthStream.

∽ WEIGHDOWN.COM

Visit our website for the most up-to-date information on coming attractions, media events, free weight loss lectures, and special events.

∽ GWENSHAMBLIN.COM

For more information on the author, Gwen Shamblin.

∽ REMNANTFELLOWSHIP.TV

"You Can Overcome"—a free interactive, LIVE online TV show hosted by Gwen Shamblin every Thursday at 11:00a.m. Central Time. Log on to watch LIVE and to see replays.

∽ REMNANTFELLOWSHIP.ORG

For more information on the Remnant Fellowship, the Church that sponsors Weigh Down Ministries, e-mail questions to info@RemnantFellowship.org.

∽ WEIGHDOWNATHOME.COM

Free Online weight loss class.

∽ WEIGHDOWNRADIO.COM

Weigh Down Web Radio (WDWB)—Free 24/7 online encouragement.

∽ WEIGHDOWNCHRONICLES.COM

Daily words from Gwen.

∽ FACEBOOK

Join the Weigh Down Ministries Facebook Group—the 24/7 newsfeed is filled with testimonies, encouragement, sharing, and answers from the office. Reach out and become a member.

∽ E-MAILS FROM WEIGH DOWN

Sign up for Weigh Down's weekly encouragement e-mails at www.WeighDown.com. They include important announcements and special discounts.

TWITTER

Follow "GwenShamblin," "WeighDown," "MichaelShamblin," and "ElizabethRFC."

YouTube

Watch inspiring videos on GwenShamblin, the Remnant Fellowship Church, MichaelShamblin, and the WeighDownWorkshop YouTube Channels.

MUSIC

For music that backs up this message and is guaranteed to turn your focus Heavenward, go to Michael Shamblin's YouTube channel, the Weigh Down online store's "Music Section," or www.MichaelShamblin.com.

For more information on these titles and seminars, please call us toll free at 1-800-844-5208 or visit our website at www.weighdown.com.

Weigh Down Ministries Local Staff
Thank you to the local Weigh Down Ministries staff and the 60 national and international Regional Representatives who work around the clock to help spread the Truth.

REMNANT FELLOWSHIP

Remnant Fellowship Churches were established in 1999 and are now in over 150 locations around the world. They sponsor world outreach to those seeking a strong connection to the One True God in these trying days and the life to come. Call 1-800-844-5208 or visit our website at www.RemnantFellowship.org.

Personal/Family Notes

Words, phrases, and thoughts that are inspiring your life:

Personal/Family Notes

Words, phrases, and thoughts that are inspiring your life:

Personal/Family Notes

Words, phrases, and thoughts that are inspiring your life:

_____

_____

_____

_____

_____

_____

_____

_____

_____

_____

_____

_____

_____

_____

_____

_____

_____

_____

_____

_____

_____

_____

_____

_____

Personal/Family Notes

Words, phrases, and thoughts that are inspiring your life:

Personal/Family Notes

Words, phrases, and thoughts that are inspiring your life:

_____

_____

_____

_____

_____

_____

_____

_____

_____

_____

_____

_____

_____

_____

_____

_____

_____

_____

_____

_____

_____

_____

_____

Personal/Family Notes

Words, phrases, and thoughts that are inspiring your life:

_____

_____

_____

_____

_____

_____

_____

_____

_____

_____

_____

_____

_____

_____

_____

_____

_____

_____

_____

_____

_____

_____

Personal/Family Notes

Words, phrases, and thoughts that are inspiring your life:

Personal/Family Notes
Words, phrases, and thoughts that are inspiring your life:

Personal/Family Notes

Words, phrases, and thoughts that are inspiring your life:

Personal/Family Notes

Words, phrases, and thoughts that are inspiring your life: